POWER TO PEOPLE

BUILDING AN ENABLING WORKPLACE CULTURE

GHANSHYAM PANT

INDIA • SINGAPORE • MALAYSIA

Notion Press

Old No. 38, New No. 6
McNichols Road, Chetpet
Chennai - 600 031

First Published by Notion Press 2019
Copyright © Ghanshyam Pant 2019
All Rights Reserved.

ISBN 978-1-64546-954-4

This book has been published with all efforts taken to make the material error-free after the consent of the author. However, the author and the publisher do not assume and hereby disclaim any liability to any party for any loss, damage, or disruption caused by errors or omissions, whether such errors or omissions result from negligence, accident, or any other cause.

No part of this book may be used, reproduced in any manner whatsoever without written permission from the author, except in the case of brief quotations embodied in critical articles and reviews.

To the three angels that have brought so much happiness in my life;

My granddaughters Arianna, Noya and Amelia.

Contents

Foreword .... *vii*

Preface .... *ix*

Acknowledgements .... *xiii*

The Beginning 1

The Challenge 5

The Approach 9

Initial Setback 13

Kanjikode Vision 19

Recruitment 29

Creating We-ness 37

The House System 51

Skill Development 59

Communication 63

Using the Community to Deal with Indiscipline 71

Involvement 77

Achievements 87

Final Words 93

Foreword

Harsh Mariwala, Chairman, Marico Limited

Ever since the birth of Marico in 1990, when the family managed business was transformed into a professionally managed business, we have tried to create a company known for its values, a belief in its people, and an appetite for risk-taking. This approach helped the company to attract and retain talent, establish a culture of innovation, and in the process grow the company both organically and inorganically. A desire for innovation finally led to the birth of the Marico Innovation Foundation, which now celebrates innovations that have positively affected economic growth.

Ghanshyam Pant joined Marico to take charge of the edible oil Plant at Jalgaon. Inspired by Marico's values, he soon started working on improving the work culture of that Plant. When it was time to establish a new factory in Kerala, we needed someone with a people orientation and project management background. Ghanshyam fit the bill. We saw many opportunities to innovate in the new factory. Some of these challenges were related to technology and processes. However, the biggest challenge was creating a culture that would counter the effect of a negative industrial climate.

This book captures what happened in Kanjikode during the time Ghanshyam was there. The narrative flows smoothly as if you are listening to a story-telling session by a 'war veteran.' He talks about his own dilemma of leaving the Jalgaon Plant without having completed the entire brief, and how he was eventually coaxed by Shreekant Gupte (Vice President Operations) to take up the job. It spells out the initial setbacks and how they were dealt with. That was, indeed, the beginning of countering many challenges proactively.

Among the most effective innovations in HR was the House System that provided leadership opportunities to the workmen members. That was a proactive solution to the challenge of unionism, a fact demonstrated by the absence of any union for a long time. There are many other examples that speak volumes about the initiatives taken to establish a truly empowering culture. The chapter on We-ness describes a number of steps taken for seamless teamwork. The example of getting Attimaris (head-load workers, with very rigid rules) to cooperate in difficult times shows how effective the approach was to engage and involve them.

Another example that made the Kanjikode culture unique was the idea of learning together. Participating in training programmes along with management staff, and co-facilitating such training helped enhance the self-esteem of the workmen members.

Ghanshyam was at the centre of all that happened in that factory. His narration comes from his own involvement in creating an empowering culture. What comes out clearly is that a shared vision can be achieved when lived by all through continuous review and dialogue.

While this book is about the steps taken in a new factory, the contents transcend those boundaries. One can use the underlying principles in any function or industry. It is a case study in culture building that can be as easily adopted as one by business schools. Leaders and HR professional, who believe in building enabling cultures, should find this book to be of significant interest. The book gives ideas about innovative approaches to be taken in the area of Human Resources. During my talks on innovation, when the audience asks me about examples of HR innovation, I quote some of the examples given in this book.

I hope the readers will find this book as engaging as I did.

(Harsh Mariwala).
April 6, 2019.

Preface

It has taken me a long time to complete this book. I first thought of writing it way back in 2003. The idea was taking shape because of the reactions I received whenever I made a presentation of the work we did in the Marico's Kerala factory during the period 1992–1996. Every time I made a presentation, gave a talk, or shared some aspects of the story informally in groups, the participants always were in awe.

One of my first presentations was at the Blue Star Corporate Office in 1996–97. I was invited by their Top Management to share our Kanjikode Culture-Building experience with their Factory Heads and HR Heads. My presentation consisted of just about 10 slides, but it took me three hours to share the experience. I still remember the applause and compliments. The MD had initially planned to stay for only a few minutes of the presentation, but he was glued to his seat right up to the end.

There were many such instances where the participants were spellbound. I wondered if the entire experience was captured in a book form, would there be many more who will get the inspiration? The inspiration of how sound people processes could help in building a great work culture! That is when I decided to give it a try.

I was wondering about the structure, contents and style of writing. Should I start with a concept and then support it with our own examples? Should I write a story without names? In the end, I decided to write it in the first person. A story as I saw and experienced it! It will have the names of all those who supported. After all, culture is built only when you have a large number of players acting in it.

So, I created the structure of the book. Each chapter was about a specific initiative. For each chapter, I wrote bullet points that would be expanded to give shape to my writing. It all looked well. A beginning had been made, and it seemed to me that the book was taking shape, but then I got too busy in my consulting work. The book took a back seat.

Months later, precisely on June 24, 2005, an article on Industrial Peace (more precisely, the lack of it) caught my attention. It was about some industries where union activities were stalling the progress of the companies. The article also made a reference to Marico Industries' Kerala Plant, which had witnessed excellent industrial relations right from its inception in 1992. That too in an industrially and politically volatile State! I was waiting at the Mumbai airport for my flight to Rajkot, but my mind raced back to a series of events that started one hot afternoon in May 1992.

I would call that 'The Beginning.' And I started writing again. I could complete that episode in one sitting, as everything was running like a movie in my mind. Now that was some progress! However, the momentum did not last long as I got busier in my work. This time years passed by without any serious attempt to continue writing the book. Thoughts also crossed my mind that perhaps people would not be interested in reading a book about something that happened over a decade ago. I was wrong.

A couple of years back I saw a video on YouTube where Harsh Mariwala, the Chairman of Marico, was talking about **innovation in HR.** He gave an example of an innovation that had been carried out in Kanjikode. I started to think that the whole story was relevant even after several years. It was about **people empowerment.** It was a story where bold steps were taken to create a strong work culture. So, I thought it was a good idea to complete the book. My consulting workload too had reduced. But I needed to reignite the spark of telling the story.

A series of reminders in the past year made me serious about completing the book. My wife Tara and my kids, Priya and Prateek, regularly encouraged me to write, now that I had some time in hand.

My past colleagues too kept asking about the progress of the book. The latest was an interaction with P. Vijayan, my friend and an ex-colleague at Marico. We were discussing along with a few HR Professionals at Rajagiri Business School, Cochin, Kerala. Vijayan and I spoke about various things that we did at Kanjikode. There was abundant interest. That is when I committed to complete the book soon. I knew, however, that recalling events that happened over 25 years ago would be a challenge. I have tried my best though.

Acknowledgements

Whom do I thank for making my first book happen, for there are many without whom I wouldn't have been able to complete it! My inspiration came from the wholehearted cooperation of all the members of Marico's Kerala factory in living and achieving the vision. This book is a tribute to everyone associated with that factory. Thank you all for your commitment and for helping me strengthen my own convictions.

My tenure at Marico was full of learning and self-development. My superiors and peers were highly supportive not only then, but even after I parted ways with the company. The credit goes to Harsh Mariwala, a leader par excellence. Thank you Harsh for reading the manuscript and writing the foreword despite your busy schedule. You have, indeed, been so supportive ever since my first day at Marico.

The story starts with a conversation with Shreekant Gupte. When I told him about my book, he was excited. He agreed to read the manuscript and gave valuable feedback. Thank you, Shreekant for your inputs and all those discussions we had that helped us live the Kanjikode Vision. Jaswant Nair, your unique thinking style and frank critique made me revisit my own assumptions during those years. I thank you for reading the manuscript and for providing me with some sharp insights.

There were many who kept on asking me to write a book on my Kanjikode experience. Among them were my clients and fellow professionals. My sincere thanks to each one of them. Special thanks to my friend Vijayan, who made me commit in front of an HR fraternity that I should publish my book before June 2019. I also thank you Vijayan, for giving me inputs in shaping the book. The fact that you, as the Dean of We School, think that the book will serve as a case study in business schools, is indeed very satisfying.

I must thank my erstwhile colleagues Nagabhushan Iyer, Ravi Nair, Srinath, Salil Raghavan, Pankaj Agarwal, Dr. Joe Lewis, Raju Sekhar and Shanto Menachery for recalling the past events to clarify my own thoughts. Thank you all for taking up my phone calls and responding promptly. Syamaprasad, though you joined Marico much later, your own assessment of the culture at Kanjikode gave me great satisfaction. Thank you for sharing your thoughts.

As I started compiling my book, I needed someone who could go through my initial drafts, and give me feedback in terms of flow and consistency. My niece, Seema Pant, did that perfectly. She would give her feedback chapter by chapter and point out obvious issues. Thank you, dear Seema. My other niece, Mukta Pant, gave me her opinion about the complete manuscript. Thank you, Micky, for the quick revert.

My daughter, Priya, insisted on reviewing the manuscript. I was reluctant because her hands were too full with her little daughters. She had experience in compiling and editing in one of the companies she had worked in the past. When I gave her the manuscript, she made a lot of suggestions, which made immense sense. She continued to help me during various stages of publishing. I thank you, dearie, for burning your midnight candles to help your dad in improving the quality of the book.

My son Prateek kept asking me from time to time about my book project. That helped my resolve to write. Thank you, Prata, for your subtle reminders, as well as your suggestion for the title.

My team at Notion Press has been very responsive. Their timely guidance helped me understand the process of publishing. I thank them for their support.

Finally, I thank my wife, Tara, who egged me on to complete this project. She firmly believes that it's just my first book and that I would be writing more. I hope I will. Thank you dear for all your support and faith in me.

The Beginning

May 1992

The place is Jalgaon in Maharashtra, where Marico had its Vegetable Oil Refinery, producing two of its popular brands Saffola Refined Kardi Oil and Sweekar Refined Sunflower Oil. The Refinery expansion was just over, but the stabilisation of the process was in progress. The excessive summer heat had created a water shortage in the city, and one of the daily meeting agenda was centred on this utility.

The morning meeting and Plant rounds were over, and I was sitting in my office when I got a call from Shreekant Gupte, Vice President Operations. Shreekant took over the Operations function in 1991. He came with rich experience in manufacturing and marketing with companies like Asian Paints, Sherin Williams and Garware Paints. He sounded excited.

"Ghanshyam, we have finalised the location for our new Parachute Coconut Oil Plant."

I responded, *"Oh really! Where? When did you decide?"*

"We made the decision today. And I decided to call you immediately. It's the most challenging decision we have taken. We are going to set up the Plant in Kerala!"

I recall our discussions during Shreekant's last visit to Jalgaon. As head of Operations, it was Shreekant's responsibility to set up the new Plant to augment the increasing market demand for the most successful brand we had, Parachute Coconut Oil, or PCNO, as it was called in short. He wanted my views about possible locations for the new Plant. The main candidates were Kerala, Karnataka and Tamil Nadu. Financially, Kerala had a definite edge over other States because of raw material advantage, but it came with a major disadvantage, industrial agitations, which severely impacted the State's industrial growth. I held the view that most industrial disputes arose because of a lack of transparent and humane approach on the part of the management. Marico, in those days, was beginning to acquire a reputation of a 'People-Oriented' company. I told Shreekant that if we pride ourselves as a company with a great human focus, we should face the challenge squarely in Kerala. In my mind, the odds were significant enough to take the decision of going there.

Shreekant agreed with my observation. And then he asked whether I would like to take that challenge and move to Kerala. As per him, my past experience in project management, together with my people-oriented approach made me the best internal candidate for the task. My immediate reaction was a firm 'No.' The Jalgaon Plant had been going through severe production related problems right since Marico acquired the old Plant over two years ago, and we were modernising the facilities to increase the capacity as well as to improve the product quality. We had taken so much flak in the past that I had no intention of leaving that place without setting things right. In my reckoning, it still required a few months to make that Plant perform at its best, and create a culture of empowerment and achievement. The people had started responding to some of the best practices in human relations. I wanted to spend another year in organisation building at Jalgaon.

Hearing him say, *"I decided to call you immediately,"* I knew what would come next.

"Well, thanks for breaking the news so soon. I really appreciate it. I am also happy at the choice of location."

"Ghanshyam, it was not an easy decision. Many friends of the Mariwala family were advising against setting up a Plant in Kerala for the most vital product of the company. It would spell doom for the company if labour problems stalled operations in the future. Having taken that decision,

it's now upon the Operations Team to make sure that we succeed. And I want you to take this challenge."

I felt a surge of excitement at the thought of creating something from nowhere, and doing it in a seemingly hostile environment made that task so much more exciting. But I was not prepared to leave this place without accomplishing my goals here. I decided to stick to my guns.

"Shreekant, thanks for offering me the role. But we have discussed this in the near past, and my stance remains unchanged. You will have to get someone else for this job. I am sorry."

"Look Ghanshyam, we have to succeed here, and I firmly believe that you are the best person for this job. I know your views and your commitment to the Jalgaon Plant. The expansion is over, and with that, the Plant will soon start performing. You have already laid the foundation for an enabling work culture. I believe Jalgaon can be managed by someone else. But the new Plant in Kerala needs you."

I was quiet for a while. Shreekant continued, *"Okay, do one thing. Take your family for a trip to Kerala. See the location in Palakkad. Show them Coimbatore. Look at the facilities for living and schooling. Then take a trip to Ooty and Mysore. After the trip, if you still feel that you don't want to go there, I will accept your decision without any argument. Is that a fair deal?"*

"Shreekant, my family is on vacation in Nainital. I am alone here."

"Take the next available flight to Delhi. Go, bring them along and take a trip to the South. All expenses paid!"

Very cleverly, Shreekant steered the discussions to counter my resistance.

The next morning, I left for Lucknow to pick up my daughter from my brother's home, and together we went to Nainital to meet my wife and son. My wife was shocked to see us. I took some time to explain the situation to her and try to get them all interested in seeing places like Bangalore, Ooty and Mysore. They were enjoying the company of relatives and friends in the beautiful hills of Kumaon, so the offer did not mean much to them. But since I had come all the way, they finally decided to take the trip.

We made the trip down South to explore the place and get a general feel of the area as this was our first trip to South India. The factory was supposed to come up in Kanjikode, an industrial town near Palakkad, Kerala. We also explored Coimbatore in the neighbouring State, Tamil Nadu, which had much better infrastructure. Every time we discussed the issue of taking the assignment; I was reminded that it had to be my decision. We enjoyed the place but deferred all decisions until we returned to Mumbai.

On our return to Mumbai, I left my family at the hotel and went to the Corporate Office to meet Shreekant. It was the third week of May 1992. We made the decision to transition Jalgaon Factory leadership to T.V. Ramachandran (from Procurement function), and I took over the responsibility of building the Kerala factory from scratch, with a specific focus on culture.

We returned to Jalgaon only to prepare ourselves for the next innings in a different place. There were farewells, some formal and others, personal. We left for Mumbai on May 30, 1992.

On June 1, 1992, this story started in Coimbatore. This story is about conviction in the power of the people. It is about trusting people and getting superior returns from their total involvement. It is about building an organisational culture that is **value-based** and driven by common **vision.** This is about revolutionary HR practices, aptly termed by Shreekant as 'path-breaking.'

The next few chapters reveal the kind of work my team carried out in the new place (with great support from Corporate) and the hugely satisfying results we were rewarded with.

The Challenge

In 1991, PCNO, the flagship brand of Marico Industries, was growing at a very healthy rate of 20% per annum. It was already a market leader and continuously increasing its market share (50% in 1991 as against 42% in 1990). The Sales and Marketing team was doing a great job and were upbeat about growth prospects. The Operations Team faced enormous challenges to keep pace with this growth. The existing facilities, consisting of Owned as well as Contracted Plants, were already running at full capacity. These old facilities would often run into quality problems leading to wastages. The writing was on the wall. If we did not add capacity, we would not be able to meet the demand. We needed to set up a new Factory with better Plant and Machinery, at a location that would be economically most feasible.

The feasibility study was conducted in 1991 by a Summer Trainee from Indian Institute of Management, Ahmedabad. The study covered various locations in the States of Maharashtra, Karnataka, Tamilnadu and Kerala.

The key results of the study were:

- Growing sales and quality issues at contract factories created a need for a new factory

- Economic feasibility heavily favoured Kerala as the best location (easy, plentiful and inexpensive availability of the raw material copra and certain tax benefits offered by the State Government)

- Environment study revealed a strongly negative industrial relations (IR) climate in Kerala. Should we take the challenge or go to safer/more conducive States?

In the end, the company's belief in sound HR practices led to the decision of setting up the factory in Kerala. The key challenge was to establish a work culture that would effectively counter the negative IR climate. This meant that right from the beginning we would have to do the right things. There was no scope for any wrong step, for the negative forces in the existing industrial climate of the State would grab the opportunity and then it would be a constant battle to right the wrong.

Kerala was known for a very high literacy rate. The people had a good awareness of their rights. Consequently, the Trade Unions were very active. Disruption of work, agitations and violence led to financial losses and sometimes closure of businesses. The Kerala Government was unable to attract fresh investments in the State. The Government announced incentives to set up industries in designated areas in the State. These incentives were lucrative. As a result, some companies gave a serious thought to setting up new factories in those areas.

However, there was another challenge! These incentives were in the form of promises made by the Industries Department. The challenge was to convert these promises to a Government Order (GO), without which claiming incentives was just not possible. To get these GOs passed, as we realised later, we would have to interact and follow up with the bureaucracy as well as the political top brass!

There was another catch to the incentives. They were for a limited period. The earlier the Plant was commissioned, the more the financial gains. So it was important to complete the project in the shortest possible time. It was also important that manpower was hired and trained to achieve the required volumes while maintaining the stringent product quality standards, and packaging vendors were persuaded to set up their units. In fact, moving selected vendors close to the new location, in itself, was a major step. They had to be convinced of the commercial viability of setting up their units in a place they had no idea about.

While the company had made its decision to set up the factory in one of the designated locations, Kerala, the vendors too needed to deal with the questions. Their biggest fear was from labour agitations in Kerala. If the organised Trade Unions started trouble either at Marico's factory or in their own, would they find it difficult to justify the investment?

All real possibilities! We could not afford a wrong foot. It had to be a highly coordinated effort.

The Approach

Having decided to invest, responsibilities were assigned for different challenges. The responsibility for getting the GO for incentives was taken by Pranab Dutta, Vice President Finance. Setting up Vendor Facilities was assigned to Shyam Sutaria, Head of Materials. Setting up sound Quality Systems, both at the new factory as well as the vendors, was taken up by the Central Quality Department under the overall leadership of Dr. Joe Lewis. My responsibilities included project management, hiring, liaison with local authorities, factory operations and above all, setting up a highly enabling **work culture**. There was a high level of support from Corporate Operations Team as well as Corporate HR.

The company had evaluated different locations in Kerala and decided to opt for Kanjikode, a small Industrial Complex in the vicinity of Palakkad. Kanjikode already had a few Industries, and it was only 40 km from Coimbatore, a prominent Industrial City in Tamil Nadu. Coimbatore had good infrastructure and availability of all kinds of resources necessary for setting up as well as running a factory.

To begin with, we set up a small project office in Coimbatore. My small team consisted of two people in project execution, an HR Head and a Commercial Head. The immediate tasks were:

- To appoint an architect for Plant layout, and design of civil and structural work
- To conduct a site-specific survey for detailed design
- To award a contract for civil and structural work

- To set up accounting systems for managing the project

- To conduct an **environmental study** of the industrial climate of Kanjikode and neighbouring areas

- To prepare a draft for **Kanjikode Vision** that would eventually build a healthy work culture

Since this book is about setting up an **enabling culture,** let me focus on the last two points. For both these, the responsibility was assigned to Suraj Aravind, our young HR Manager. He immediately started with a detailed survey of industries in the neighbourhood. He made a list of all the industries present within a 20 km radius. Most of these were in the Kanjikode Industrial Estate. Some, like Malabar Cement, were away.

The study comprised of meeting the location heads and HR heads of these industries to understand the following focal points:

1. The demographic profile of workers, including data on their age, gender and community they belonged to

2. Labour availability

3. Trade Union presence

4. History of labour trouble

5. People Initiatives

6. Wage Structure

7. Welfare facilities like canteen, transportation, uniforms, medical, etc.

8. Success stories and failures

9. Relationship with neighbouring industries

10. Relationship with neighbouring communities

In addition to the above, we decided to meet people in the neighbouring community to understand their viewpoints. Suraj diligently and doggedly pursued the task, meeting people daily and making detailed notes. He was ably supported by our Commercial Head Ravi Nair, a highly experienced Chartered Accountant who lived in Palakkad after returning from the Middle East. At the end of each day, I would review the findings with Suraj, and discuss if any additional inputs were required. At times he would ask me to meet certain location heads to understand their perspective better.

Suraj was fresh from Xavier Labour Relations Institute (XLRI), Jamshedpur. He was sharp and hard working. In the beginning, he appeared daunted by the mammoth task. However, thanks to our daily reviews, he soon got wholly immersed in the task at hand. He realised that he had received an opportunity that very few get at the beginning of their career. That in itself was a great motivation for him.

Suraj also did manpower studies on Marico's Mumbai factory and the Coconut Oil Mills in Kerala.

The findings of the study were to be used for manpower planning, recruitment, wage structure, welfare plans and engagement initiatives. This gave birth to the first draft of **Kanjikode Vision.** It was a very detailed draft that included not only our aspirations but also the do's and don'ts for achieving it.

Initial Setback

Attimari Issues Impacting Construction

The initial project work started. The architect was engaged, a site survey was conducted to understand the soil conditions and water table, and a Civil Contractor was appointed for carrying out the civil and structural work.

The civil work started with the construction of temporary facilities and the basic infrastructure of boundary walls, fences and internal roads. That is when we had our first experience with Kerala's famous labour union agitation! Here we were confronted by Attimari Unions, who staked their claim for doing the head-load work at their rates.

Who Are Attimaris?

I asked James, our Civil Contractor, "Who are Attimaris?" From what we understood from him, they were like the *Mathadis* in Maharashtra, who not only specialised in carrying out head-load work but would not allow any company to deploy its own labour for such activities. These activities included all loading and unloading activities. We already had experience with the Mathadi Unions in our factories in Maharashtra. Like them, the Attimaris were very adamant people, known for disrupting work if their demands were not met.

Our construction activities, which had barely started, came to a halt. James thought that we should not entertain them, and evict them from their *Dharna* (sit out agitation in front of the premises) with the help of the Police. Which, of course, we did. The Police would come and disperse them. They would come again. This agitating group of Attimaris was controlled by the Bharatiya Mazdoor Sangh (BMS) Union, one of the many Trade Unions operating in the area. We decided to meet the union leaders.

In the first meeting, we asked them to state their demands. The Attimaris were among the lowest educated in Kerala, but their leader was well-educated and behaved well to a large extent. The union demanded that all loading and unloading activities would be conducted only by the union members, and for every activity, the rates would be set by the union. We listened to their demands but also pointed to them that while their demands were not acceptable, we would still study the norms, and meet again. Obviously, they were not happy.

Based on our internal meetings and consultation with the Corporate Office, we decided to offer the Attimaris head-load work for **unloading** all materials other than raw materials and packaging materials, and **loading** of all finished goods, by-products, and other materials going out of the factory. We also compared the rates with existing standards in other industries, as well as our own budget estimates.

In the following meetings, we stated our intention of not using the Attimaris for anything related to raw materials and packaging materials. We told them we could use their services for finished goods, which was substantial in volume. We even gave them a fair idea of the work involved. They could also carry out unloading activities in our general stores, and loading for any material going out of the factory. After some deliberations, they realised the scope of work was large and accepted our offer. Next, we negotiated on the rates. We told them that their rates were too high. The net income per person, based on their productivity, was far higher than the State's minimum wages. However, they did not want to budge. We asked them to think again and come back to the negotiating table. A couple of meetings later, we agreed to their revised rates. They also spelt out their rules for loading and unloading activities. These were:

- All their activities will be from 9:00 a.m. to 5:00 p.m. If a truck is not entirely loaded or unloaded by 5:00 p.m., the remaining work would be done the next morning. In other words, they wanted us to plan well, and not start an activity close to the end of the day.

- No work on Sundays and public holidays.

We accepted these rules as these were manageable issues. From our side, we put a condition that the Attimaris would only enter the premises for work. If there was no loading or unloading activity, all the union members would stay outside the gate. They agreed to this condition, and the agreement was signed.

This set to rest the agitation and our construction activities picked up momentum. Just when we thought it was all over, we found to our dismay another agitation started by a different Attimari Union. Imagine what must have been the reason!

These Attimari Unions were very organised. They had a clear demarcation of territories. Now it so happened that the milestone that marked the operating boundary of two unions was right in the middle of the premises. So far all loading and unloading activities were happening in the area which was on one side of the Milestone. Our general store was on the other side. The day material handling started at this store, some members of the other Attimari Union noticed the activity and came in large numbers to agitate. We had to take the help of the cops to disperse the crowd.

However, the agitation would continue. Every day, the agitators would come, and then the Police would take them away in buses. The slogan-shouting made our staff a bit nervous. There were two opinions. One opinion was to ignore them. The other was to have a dialogue and resolve the issues. I agreed to the second. So we met these guys and heard them. We asked them their expectations. They said since the work areas for the two groups were clearly demarked, there will not be any issue between the two. Further, they would agree with whatever rates the company had agreed with the BMS group. After some discussions on norms of behaviour and other conditions, we agreed to them. The BMS group had no objection to this agreement.

This was a good beginning. Attimaris in Kerala have a negative image. There were many operations in different parts of the State that were severely impacted. Companies lost money and business in this tussle. We made a point that we would not allow this to happen at our premises. To achieve that we took some heart winning steps later, and the results were very encouraging.

This experience reminded me of my conversation with a Malayali gentleman while returning from Trivandrum a few weeks earlier. I was on one of my routine visits to the State capital to follow up on certain project approvals. On my return journey, my co-passenger was a Malayali. We struck a conversation. He told me that he worked in Bengaluru, and was returning after a brief vacation in his hometown. Then he asked me about my purpose of visiting Kerala. I told him about the project and that the land had just been acquired from the Kerala State Industrial Development Corporation (KSIDC). The moment I said that, his reaction was unbelievable.

"Are you mad?"

I was taken aback and asked him the reason for such a strong reaction.

"You will lose all your investments. You must pack your bags and set up a Plant elsewhere. If you leave now, you will only lose the investment in the land. Otherwise, after a year when you would have invested more money in Plant and Machinery, and hired people, the labour unions will agitate so hard that you will have to go back. At that time your loss will be much more. Go back now. Forget investing in Kerala."

I asked him how a person from Kerala could ask someone not to invest in his State. Wasn't it strange? He did have his reasons.

"Why do you think that most Malayalis work outside the State? Why do you think I am working in a neighbouring State? There are so many negative forces in our State who don't allow businesses to prosper in the State. You still have time. Go back."

We agreed to disagree. I told him to follow the progress of our project and operations in the coming months and years. I assured him that he would soon change his views, after what we achieve with our investment.

In my mind, I stored the whole conversation. I wanted it to serve as a reminder so that we achieve our goals.

Kanjikode Vision

We believed that sustainable work culture can only be established if everyone in the organisation is aligned. For that, we needed a starting point. So, in our endeavour to build an enabling culture at Kanjikode, we decided to first co-create a vision for the factory.

At the corporate level, Marico had a mission and a set of well-articulated values. As an organisation, Marico was just over two years old, having transitioned from a family managed business to a professionally managed one. A large number of senior and middle-level managers were hired from different companies with a diverse background. It was Harsh's foresight that he decided to co-create Marico's Mission and Values along with the entire top and senior management. Vice President HR, Jeswant Nair, orchestrated the efforts with zeal. Jeswant, a graduate from XLRI, Jamshedpur had earlier worked with Asian Paints and Blue Dart Express. He steered the entire organisation in implanting sound HR practices. Thanks to several initiatives, Marico soon established its unique culture.

Learning from Marico's success with building a unique work culture, we decided to conduct a Vision Workshop, which was attended by all five members of my team and Shreekant. Jeswant facilitated the workshop. Every member was provided with a report collated by Suraj based on Industrial Environment data collected. The idea was to bring everyone on the same page about the existing situation so that the collective viewpoints could be processed during the Vision Workshop.

The key points of Suraj's Report were:

- There were multiple unions in the neighbouring industries.

- Most of the older factories had witnessed agitations, and the management in these factories were wary of the unions.

- One of the recently established factories had deployed only female labour. The Factory Head of this Textile Spinning factory strongly suggested that we hire female labour who were not aggressive.

- Welfare measures included canteen and uniform and varied from company-to-company. Providing a canteen facility was more of a necessity as the Industrial Area was remote. The report also suggested welfare measures that could be adopted.

- Minimum wages drove the pay in the beginning. However, once the unions were formed, the wages were negotiated based on the Charter of Demand (COD). Suraj suggested a wage structure in his report based on minimum wages, as well as existing wages in some factories. He also took into account the type of skills required.

- The communication between the management and the workers was mostly through the **Union Representatives.** There was no proactive approach to communicate. The report also suggested some of the initiatives to promote regular two-way communication.

- There was no structured approach to building a culture or a sense of belonging. The report suggested measures that could help in creating a culture of 'We-ness.'

- A local Management Association was the apt place for discussing issues and served as a significant source of sharing knowledge.

- Availability of both skilled and unskilled labour was good. While the adjoining areas within the district had plenty of resources for unskilled labour recruitment, the skilled labour needed to be sourced from adjoining districts as well.

- KSIDC was improving the infrastructure, and there were plans for starting regular bus services to our factory location.

- The corporate support for community activities was little.

The key questions we needed to answer was *'What is it that we wanted to achieve at the Kanjikode Factory?'* and *'How should we go about it?.'* In order to answer this, we chose to co-create a ***vision.***

A ***vision*** is a state of the future destination we aim for. As we brainstormed, several images came to our minds, including the one that our factory could be the model factory in the country! Wasn't that too ambitious? We were reminded of two fundamental principles of defining a Vision Statement.

- The vision must be exciting. It should not be too easy to achieve.

- The vision must be achievable. It must not be so difficult that people stop believing in it.

It is like tuning a guitar. If the string tension is too less, there will not be any music. If the tension is too much, the string may break. The right amount of tension alone can produce great music. The vision should be such that people can achieve it with reasonable stretch, and when they do, they will derive a great deal of pleasure.

After considerable discussions, we concluded that we should aim to make the Kanjikode Factory a model (a Touchstone/Standard) not only in Kerala but among all factories of Marico nationwide. That sounded exciting and achievable, albeit with substantial efforts.

The statement read as follows:

"We would like to build a factory and organisation that will serve as a model within Marico and Kerala."

That done, the next task was to enumerate 'how.' Jeswant said we should identify the Pillars of our vision. Pillars that will not only help achieve our vision but also support it. While identifying the Pillars, we also kept in mind Marico's Mission and Values. The team decided on the following five Pillars:

1. **Culture:** To create highly engaged and empowered work teams through a focus on People, Products and Processes

2. **Aesthetics:** The focus was on a green environment and good housekeeping

3. **Reliability:** With a focus on Customer, this Pillar would promote quality and delivery of products

4. **External Image:** To build an External Image that would make us known as a responsible corporate citizen, and be a preferred employer and business partner

5. **Continuous Improvement:** To create an internal environment where everyone is engaged in the continual improvement of work methods and processes

At the end of the first Vision Workshop, we had a draft Vision Statement together with its Pillars. It was decided to flesh this draft, as well as add meat to the Pillars, in terms of how the whole implementation would be done. We agreed to meet again for another two-day workshop to give the vision a final shape.

Post the Workshop, Suraj worked on various aspects. Where required, he took input from other members of the team, and at times, from the HR fraternity within the organisation. He would discuss the drafts with me at length. After several iterations, we thought we were ready for the second Workshop. By this time, we had a few more people in our team.

The Kanjikode Vision draft was discussed threadbare. It did not take much time to agree on the first statement of our vision. Most of the time was consumed in discussing the details of the Pillars. After all, achieving a vision is like completing a project, and every project must be detailed enough to ensure smooth execution.

While each of the five Pillars was important, it was the Culture Pillar that required maximum focus. In this, we discussed everything from Recruitment to Training to Communication to Recognition, and so on.

We also coined an acronym for Kanjikode Vision. It was called 'Continuous CARE.' This acronym was to help everyone remember the essence of the Vision. While the word 'Continuous' represented the Pillar Continuous Improvement, the word 'CARE' represented the other four Pillars. C was for Culture, A was for Aesthetics, R was for Reliability, and E was for External Image. 'Continuous CARE,' in essence, also represented an attitude of ongoing care for all our resources. It was a great acronym!

After a few more iterations, the Kanjikode Vision document was finally produced. Now officially, 'Continuous CARE' was born. The whole document was in two parts: The Kanjikode Vision, a two-page document, followed by a detailed 'Vision to Practice' document that ran into several pages.

The final Vision read as follows:

Kanjikode Vision

We Would Like to Build a Factory and Organisation Which Will Serve As a Prototype Within Marico and Kerala. We Would Seek to Do This by Specifically Focusing on Five Pillars.

1. ***CULTURE***

    We would be known for a superior quality of people, products and processes. We will build a work culture where people engage in healthy relationships and where work teams and people are empowered to decide and act in the best interest of the company.

2. ***AESTHETICS***

    We would ensure that the Plant and its surroundings are well laid out and landscaped. We shall emphasise on greenery and vegetation in the State. We would ensure that the workstations, manufacturing processes and people habits reflect a high degree of hygiene and safety.

3. ***RELIABILITY***

    We would endeavour to make products that time and again meet the requirements of the consumers, both in terms of quality and quantity. We will develop technologies and processes that would help us deliver to the consumer a product that has a few equals. We will deploy our resources in a manner that ensures the most efficient cost structure in the industry.

4. ***EXTERNAL IMAGE***

    We will be known as an enlightened organisation and as a responsible corporate citizen. We will attract and nurture some of the best talent available in the neighbourhood and our business associates share a privileged relationship with us. Our Government and public relations ensures support for all of our programs and business activities.

5. ***CONTINUOUS IMPROVEMENT***

    We will design our work methods and processes in a manner that helps us make continuous, day-to-day improvements, however small, in everything that we do; even though we may already have established high standards.

The intelligence and energies that would go into realising this vision of a model factory and organisation can best be summed up by the phrase "Continuous CARE".

Living the Vision

Finalising a Vision Statement and documenting it was just the beginning. We were fully aware that unless we consciously work on it, the vision will only remain on paper. So we decided to follow 'Vision to Practice' in a disciplined manner. Much of the remaining parts of this book detail the various steps taken by the Kanjikode Team. At this stage, when we had just finalised the Vision, we knew that we would have to focus on the following:

1. Ensure that every member was well versed with the Kanjikode Vision, and would relate every activity with 'Continuous CARE.' To achieve this, we conducted several one-day 'Vision Workshops.' The objective of these workshops was to familiarise the members with the Kanjikode Vision and 'Continuous CARE' Pillars. Discussions included how best to practice these Pillars. Members would offer examples of their work areas. These workshops left a strong impression in their minds. Some of the members had their close relatives working in other companies. They were aware that such a vision focused culture was absent in those companies. This made them feel proud and helped them assimilate the true spirit of the vision.

   What Gets Reviewed, Gets Improved

   To further strengthen their belief in the vision, Departmental Heads would ask the members to relate their work activities with the vision Pillars. On my Plant rounds, I would ask individuals, "Which Pillar did you strengthen today?" For me, it had become a habit to ask this question. Everyone knew that. They would be ready with their example. Sometimes, I would ask them to explain further if I was not convinced. That helped because it made people understand the actual meaning of each Pillar. I loved the examples they would give. Below is an example of a conversation I had with one of our supervisory staff:

"Tell me Suresh, which Pillar did you strengthen today?"

"Sir, I strengthened the Pillar, External Image."

"What did you do?"

"When I was coming to the factory, I gave my seat in the bus to a lady."

"Shouldn't we be doing that anyway? It's civilised behaviour. What has that got to do with our Pillar, External Image?"

"Sir, I was in my company uniform. When I gave the seat to the lady, people must have seen that a Marico employee gave the seat. So it must have improved our company's image."

What a way to see the vision in practice! To me, that reflected their complete association with the vision.

2. Get into doing the right things. We successfully experimented with several initiatives. However, before implementation, we focused on small details to ensure that we did not run into starting problems. The key was people involvement. We involved people in the planning as well as execution stages of every initiative.

3. Provide adequate training for each member. Employees came from diverse backgrounds. Apart from skill training to carry out their respective jobs, they needed training in soft skills and Total Quality Management (TQM). It had to be a structured process. To begin with, we decided on a training man-day's goal, and accordingly did the manpower planning. This ensured that each member would necessarily go through a minimum of seven days' training without affecting their day-to-day work. We did have to

put up explanations for the manpower budget. Since the logic was in line with our Vision, we did not have great difficulty in getting the approvals.

4. We ensured that 'Continuous CARE' became central to all our programmes and activities. Whether it was a departmental meeting, a workshop, training, or our annual communication exercise, we would associate the topics of discussion with one or more Pillars. Even when there was a change of leadership in 1996, we made sure that there was a formal handing over of Kanjikode Vision. It reflected the resolve of the new Factory Head to the Kanjikode Vision.

In hindsight, all those thoughtful actions proved right. Marico Kanjikode was firmly on its way to achieving the vision.

Recruitment

Any new factory raises a host of expectations among various stakeholders. The local population hopes to get jobs for the unemployed. The politicians look at it as a source to enhance their clout. The owners are apprehensive about the quality of people, both in terms of attitude and aptitude.

To begin with, we first set the norms for recruitment. We discussed novel methods of sourcing, selection and induction. We also gave adequate thought to deal with external pressures.

Norms for Recruitment

Suraj's study of the neighbouring industries was the basis for setting up recruitment norms. We learnt a lot from the factories that were set up in the immediate past. There was one company that had gone for an almost 'all-women workforce.' The Factory Head emphasised that women workers were less likely to create trouble. However, that factory was in textile spinning, where deftness of hands was an important criterion, in which women excelled. The type of work in our factory required physical strength. The conditions would not have attracted women workers. So, we decided to go for all-male workers.

The key guidelines for recruitment were:

- **Young Candidates:** Must be below 20 years for the unskilled category. The maximum limit for the skilled category was 30 years.
- **Stable Family:** Family background check must reveal that there were no issues of crime and unwanted social behaviour.

- Economically needy candidates would get preference.

- Every candidate would have to go through a structured Selection Process. There was no scope for showing favouritism.

- Ensure a mix of 80:20 for unskilled workers. 80% should be from local areas within a radius of 15–20 km, while 20% would be from far off places. Even those from a 15 km radius would be from all the directions. The idea was to have a well-distributed workforce in the region.

- Match the demography of the area, in terms of religion.

- Since Palakkad area had sizeable Tamilians, the target recruitment was in a ratio of 25% Tamil and 75% Malayalees.

- **Qualifications:** Unskilled must have passed SSLC, while the skilled must possess ITI qualification.

- Avoid candidates with political affiliation.

A Novel Method for Sourcing

The next step was to get applications from the target geographies. It is easier to say that we will have representations from different parts. In reality, the chances were that most applications would come from people who had some kind of connection with those already working in the Industrial Area. So, our first step was to communicate with all people living in the target areas within the 15 km radius.

We wanted to ensure that people understood our intent clearly. Our communication must address the following:

- Age and qualification requirements
- Selection process elements
- No scope for any referrals—political or otherwise

The communication was in the form of a pamphlet in Malayalam.

The easiest way was to just send it to homes along with the newspapers. That, however, would not have ensured wide distribution. So, Suraj's team decided to visit all the villages in the target geography. They met the village elders and distributed the pamphlets. It was also an opportunity to connect with the local population. Now people were getting to know Marico. No one had ever come to their villages, asking them to send candidates for selection. Here was a different company. The message was clear that the selection would be on merit and no amount of political pressure would help. The subtle message was that any recommendation would serve as a disqualification. As a result, we received a large number of applications.

Countering Political and Other Pressures

Despite our direct communication, some people believed that getting jobs would be easier if there was a recommendation from political heavyweights. So while they applied, they also sought recommendations from the local politicians. Typically these would be in the form of a telephone call.

Suraj, armed with our recruitment policy of not yielding to any pressure, would tell those politicians upfront that recommendations were not welcome. His response would often upset the caller. After a few calls, Suraj was exasperated and brought to my notice one particular caller who was being difficult to handle. We decided that Suraj would continue to take the call and politely tell the person about the Selection Process. If the caller became aggressive, he would ask him to talk to me.

I reflected on the situation. Typically, such a caller makes the call right in front of the person who came to him for a recommendation. He wants to impress the person about his power by speaking in a forceful voice on the phone. He cannot take a 'No' for a response from the other side. In all probability, he forgets about the whole conversation after the candidate has left.

There was no point in getting into a confrontation with these powerful people. Even if we were right, they could always create some difficulties. So, we decided not to antagonise them. I called this person and told him about our recruitment drive and the process. I sought his help to ask eligible candidates to apply. I also told him that we would give preference to his recommended candidates after they had qualified. He agreed that it was a good idea to have a structured, merit-based process. The approach helped. However, he would call me every time a Written Test was conducted. He would give the application number of the candidates. Every time I would tell him that we would give the preference if the candidate qualified.

Later, I started calling him after the process to communicate where the candidate failed. I used to request him to send better candidates. I think this approach worked well. We were asking him for more candidates instead of telling him just 'No.' Our entire team was happy that we were able to recruit people without succumbing to any pressure.

Selection Process

The key thinking in the organisation was that we had to be much more rigorous about the selection of workers (who did not enjoy mobility) compared to the selection of engineers and managers (where wrong recruitment was correctable). Our Selection Process consisted of a Written Test, a Psychological Test, Preliminary Interview by a Team of Departmental Heads, Skill/Weight Test, Final Interview by me, Medical Examination and Reference Check. These are elaborated below.

- **Written Test:** The Written Test consisted of General Knowledge, Basic Knowledge of Arithmetic and English. While the process related information was planned to be provided in Malayalam, it was necessary that the workmen members should be able to read product and package information without difficulty. Basic knowledge of arithmetic was to ensure that the worker could do simple arithmetical functions as a part of his job.

- **Psychological Test:** In the Jalgaon Plant of Marico, we had engaged the services of a Psychologist Social Worker who created a profile for every worker. It was a useful analysis, and we wanted to introduce it here. However, we were unable to locate a suitable resource. We discussed our objective and prejudices. There was a fear that the unskilled work, which involved hard manual labour, would be resisted. The workers would have to lift 50 kg bags, stack them, open and empty them out. They would also be required to physically carry packaged goods.

  As per the demography we were likely to have a majority of people from upper caste communities who probably would resent such manual work. We wanted to break this prejudice against manual labour. Our strategy was to show a video clip of the work carried out at our Mumbai factory. This 15-minute session was included along with the Written Test. The video clearly showed workers lifting heavy bags on their backs and crates of the finished product on their shoulders. While the video was played, invigilators would note the expression on the faces of the candidates. They would note if anyone had a feeling of disgust on their face.

  This method worked very well as we were able to judge if anyone had a dislike for such manual work. The bigger learning from this experiment was that most people had no objection to carrying loads. It was just a myth that was broken.

- **Preliminary Interview by HODs:** The HOD team consisted of the Commercial Manager, Production Manager and the HR Head. They rated the candidate on various aspects of his attitude, communication capability, teamwork orientation, his family background, his schooling and his understanding of the work he was expected to do.

- **Skill/Weight Test:** The skilled category candidates would be tested for their basic skills, while the unskilled category candidates would go through a weight test. The idea of a weight test was taken from a story told by a guide in the Padmanabhapuram Palace. It was the capital of the erstwhile Kingdom of Travancore. Inside the Palace grounds, there is a heavy roundish stone object. The guide narrated that the stone was used to test the strength of soldiers. True or false, the idea stuck in my mind. We decided to include this test. The shortlisted candidates were asked to pick a 50 kg bag of copra (our raw material) on their back and then walk for about 25 meters. They used to do it with a smile.

- **Final Interview by General Manager (Works):** After HODs' recommendation, the candidate would finally be seen by me. I took as much as one hour to interview each candidate. Sometimes, even longer. I used the opportunity to create a connection with the person. I did not know Malayalam, and the candidates could hardly communicate in English. Yet, we were able to understand each other. It is very difficult to explain how exactly we communicated. I guess it was more of 'heart-to-heart' communication that did not depend on language proficiency. After one particular batch of final interviews, Ravi came to my cabin.

    "Ghanshyam, we were wondering about your interviews with the candidates. You take almost one hour. How do you communicate? What exactly is your mode of communication?"

    "Well Ravi, let me ask you something. You remember the candidate who is an expert in Kalaripayattu?"

    "Yes, you are talking about Renjith! He is an expert in this form of Martial Arts."

    "Do you know he had a fight with some boys in his school?"

    "No, I don't."

    "Well there were some boys who were teasing a girl, and this boy challenged them. He used his Kalaripayattu skills to teach them a lesson."

"Okay. Now I know that you are really able to converse with the candidates. Remarkable indeed!"

It would have been great if I had learnt Malayalam. The young boys were so full of enthusiasm; I would have enjoyed the conversation even more. Nevertheless, I felt a sense of satisfaction after each interview. I learnt a lot about their family, their interests and their passion.

- **Medical Checks** were standard. Ours being an edible oil industry, it was necessary to ensure that the selected candidates were in good health and did not have any contagious disease.

- **Reference Checks:** For reference checks, someone from the HR Team would go to the candidate's village or town, meet key people in the neighbourhood (e.g. village elders) to ascertain the behaviour of the candidate. This method of reference checks also provided us with an opportunity to explain to them the kind of company their wards would be working for.

Our Recruitment Process was so rigorous that we got the best available people to join our team. The recruitment ratio was about 1:9 (one selection per nine applications). It was very important to do this first step right.

Induction

We believed that a structured induction would help the candidates to understand and assimilate the culture of the company they were joining. By the time the candidates were selected, they already had a good idea of the company through video and multiple interviews. Immediately on selection, they were taken through a one-week Induction Programme. Each day was structured. One half of the day would be an Induction Session, while in the other half, they would be engaged in work in their designated department. The idea was not to make it a continuous 'Classroom' activity. That would have been boring. Additionally, the other half day in the workplace allowed them to discuss what they learnt in the classroom.

The Induction Sessions included briefing on the following:

- History of the company, its performance record and its Products
- Organisation Structure, Introduction to People
- Standing Orders of the Factory
- Culture of the Organisation; Marico's Values
- Personnel Policies of the Factory
- Concepts of Safety, Quality and Productivity
- Leaves, Wages, Timings and whom to report, etc.
- Discipline expected in the Factory
- Description of the Work Flow and Plant Visits
- Visits to the Market along with Company Sales Representative (facilitated by Area Sales Manager, who was part of the National Sales Team)
- Kanjikode Vision

It will not be wrong to say that the Recruitment Process was very successful. The entire Kanjikode Team was proud of this process. I must acknowledge the role played by the Corporate HR Team as well as the valuable inputs provided by the HR Managers of the Mumbai and Jalgaon Plants.

Creating We-ness

Culture is about how we behave collectively, what are the unique things we do together, what are our common values, and so on. There is always a pattern others can see. At the corporate level, Marico had already done substantial work in creating a culture of openness. Marico's values, the three Ps (People, Products, Profits), were quite well-defined, and there were multiple values workshops to ensure that these values were practised.

We identified the need to create a sense of **We-ness** among all members of the Kanjikode works team. This was absolutely important if we wanted to have a strongly-bonded organisation that would negate the effect of an Industrial climate of distrust and disruption that existed in Kerala. We took several initiatives, some of which were time-tested and picked up from successful organisations, and others that were developed as we experienced actual implementation. The spirit of **Continuous Improvement,** one of the Pillars of Kanjikode Vision, was always present in implementing and refining these initiatives.

Common Uniform for All

Introducing uniforms was not a novel idea. Many factories implemented it. However, only a few succeeded in using this as a means to build a **We-ness.** I remember seeing an interview of the CEO of a successful company, where even the MD wore the same uniform as the workers. He talked about uniformity across levels through uniforms. Great! Why should we not implement it with the same spirit?

We did have uniforms in all the Marico factories. However, we decided to design our own uniforms. The first year, we decided on two types of uniforms: one for the workers, a dark-coloured uniform, and the other for the management staff, a light-coloured shirt and dark-coloured trousers. Everyone seemed to be happy. However, the different uniforms did not necessarily reflect our intention of creating **We-ness.**

In the first Annual Organisational Communication Exercise (OCE) that year, the Top Management team was addressing the entire Kanjikode team in one of the Plant buildings. When I looked at the assembly from the dais, I could see the management staff was sitting in a separate group. The light-coloured uniform clearly differentiated them from those wearing the dark-coloured uniform! It was clear that we would fail to leverage the power of the uniform, if we did not do something about it.

Post the Workshop, the Kanjikode Management Team (KMT) met and discussed implementing a common uniform. As was our process, we wanted to involve more people in the decision making, so that there was no resistance. Our management staff was in love with their uniform. They did not want any change. How do we break this mindset? Their view was that dark uniform was fine for Plant-related work, where there was a chance of soiling. Their own job was supervisory, and there was no possibility of soiling. We heard them patiently, reserving our final decision. The last thing we wanted was to force the decision.

I asked our administration executive to call the tailor for stitching one uniform for me. We decided to keep it a secret. A week later, I came to the factory in the new uniform, a dark-coloured outfit. As I walked in and took Plant rounds, the workmen members would look at me and give me knowing smiles. I allowed the impression to sink in their minds. In the evening, I called some of the management staff and asked them about their impression. I told them I would continue in the same uniform and that they were welcome to join me. They all smiled and agreed. Sometimes, the solution to a problem is that simple!

The sight of everyone in the same dark-grey uniform did help in creating a feeling of **We-ness.**

Everyone wearing the same uniform was an inspiring sight. I remember Raj Aggarwal, then Vice President Marketing, telling me how he liked that concept. A couple of years later when Raj became Vice President Operations (as a part of the Job Rotation policy of the company), the first thing he asked me was one set of Kanjikode uniform. Whenever he visited the Kanjikode factory, he would wear that uniform.

Card Punching for All

In those days the attendance was recorded through **card punching** for workmen members and **muster signing** for management staff members. That was another class creator. So, we decided to have **card punching** as a common system for all. The advent of technology made it easier to monitor attendance. It helped in identifying the latecomers. We hardly had any major issue, but through timely counselling, we got rid of a potential problem.

Eating Together – Eating the Same Food

In the beginning, we did not think of making any food other than tea available to our members, until our canteen building was ready. We had just one small pantry in the office. For the Plants, we provided some basic equipment and utensils. The Plant personnel would take necessary consumables like milk and sugar from the pantry, and prepare their own tea. The responsibility for cleaning and maintaining the equipment was with the workers, who would rotate the duty among themselves. Preparing tea and drinking it together with the Plant management staff would be a good relaxing activity.

The canteen building was taking shape. It was time to decide how to run the canteen, what should be the subsidy, etc. We were aware that if not managed well, the canteen would become a perennial source of grievance. The KMT decided to follow a different approach.

The rules were:

- The canteen will be managed completely by a committee consisting of both workers and management staff members. The committee will have the authority to appoint (and fire, if necessary) a contractor, decide on the menu, print and manage the coupons, keep an account to ensure timely payment to the contractor, etc. In other words, the company had no role at all.

- For the subsidy, the rule was simple. The company would pay 50% of the contractor's bill. There was no cap for the cost of each meal. We gave full freedom to the committee to decide whatever menu they wanted. Since every individual would have to bear 50% of the cost, there was no chance of the total cost going out of hand.

- Everyone, from top to bottom, will eat the same food.

- Food will not be cooked inside the premises. Cooking could lead to hygiene issues, which an edible oil Plant could ill afford.

- Everyone will eat from the plate provided by the company, and keep it in their respective lockers after cleaning.

The committee was formed, and with the guidance of the HR Department, it started functioning. The first task was to hire a contractor. However, before that, they needed to know what should be the menu, how many would eat lunch or dinner, and how much was each member willing to pay. After extensive consultations with members in each Plant during the shift meetings, they finally knew the extent of the contractor's scope. They called for quotations, had many discussions with the bidders, and finally selected a contractor.

The first contractor did not last long. The committee was dissatisfied with the quality of food. So, they hired another contractor and fired the first. It took the committee around six months to stabilise the whole process. The third contractor seemed to meet all the requirements. I think the committee members felt enriched by their role and the responsibility assigned to them. To their credit, they interacted well with the masses and ensured that quality food was made available to them.

While we were talking about each person cleaning their plate after eating, there was a mention of another myth. Some said that the members (both management staff and workers) would find the plate washing a menial task, and would not want to do this. After all, in other factories, the contractors did all the cleaning. We were, however, convinced that the act of washing the plates would further help in creating a sense of **We-ness**. We wanted to break this myth. We decided that on the very first day of the canteen services, I along with other members of KMT would be the first to wash our plates in the sink. Watching their General Manager and the HODs will have a positive impact, and the resistance, if any, would melt away.

Being part of the canteen opening was a matter of priority for me. However, on that day, I was required to be in the Corporate Office in Mumbai for a very important work. I asked Ravi to personally ensure that he was the first one to clean his plate. Ravi was our second in command. His vocation as a Chartered Accountant had made him highly process-oriented. He was the one who inaugurated the canteen, and after eating very happily cleaned his plate. Others saw him with respect, and after that, it was just a routine for everyone to do their own cleaning.

Learning Together, Teaching Together

To create a high sense of **We-ness,** we were continuously looking for opportunities. We soon found one in training. As an organisation, Marico had implemented the concepts of Kaizen, Housekeeping and Visual Factory. These were the concepts that everyone in the company was taught. In other factories of our company, there were separate training modules for workers and management staff. We saw this as an opportunity to further strengthen **We-ness.** We decided to have a mix of workmen members and management staff members in these workshops. Initially, there was some resistance at the corporate level, but it soon vanished when they understood our intent.

We had a Training Hall that could accommodate around 20 people. Every batch consisted of about 15 workmen members and five staff members. The workers were quite surprised to see their superiors sitting alongside them and learning together. The word spread out. There was a different sense of **We-ness.** *So far, we were wearing the same uniform and eating the same food, and now we are learning together! It was like we were all classmates!* After that, there were more batches.

We went one step further. We decided to ask the participants of the workshop to volunteer for co-facilitating the future workshops. Some volunteers were selected after evaluating their performance in the workshop. Subsequently, each workshop would have a worker as a co-facilitator.

In one of the batches, I sat through two days along with others learning the same things as they did. One of the workshop's co-facilitator was a worker. Imagine the pride he had in explaining the concepts to the General Manager!

Later, whenever there were visitors to the Plant, we would make a small team consisting of staff and workers to take them through the Plants. The workers proudly conducted the tour. The visitors too felt impressed.

This whole experiment of learning and teaching together was a grand success. It further cemented the bond between the workers and the staff members. We were finally creating the culture we had envisioned.

Social Functions

One of the most effective ways to create a sustainable **We-ness** is to celebrate together. Social functions are deeply ingrained in our DNA.

In Kerala, celebrations go beyond religious affiliation. Even though Onam is a Hindu festival, all communities in the State take part in the celebrations. It is a State festival, without any doubt. When we talked about which social functions could be celebrated together, the obvious choice was Onam.

In our very first year, we formed a committee to make preparations for Onam celebrations. Typically, the festival is celebrated over a period of three to four days. This is an occasion for people to go home and celebrate with their families. The committee members spoke to all the workers and staff members and convinced them to celebrate the festival together inside the factory premises. It was not a difficult job to do. The Kanjikode Vision Pillar 'Culture' was the driving force. Everyone, without any exception or reservation, wholeheartedly supported the idea.

There were two key events, as part of the celebration. The first was *'Pookkalam,'* which involved making various flower arrangements with different varieties of flowers. The second was *'Onam Sadhya,'* a lavish feast consisting of several vegetarian dishes. The Pookkalam would take most of the morning, followed by Sadhya, after which everyone could go home to join their family celebrations. Everyone was willing to give half a day of their official holiday to celebrate together inside the factory. I hoped that the events were executed well so that everyone felt it was a worthwhile celebration. The committee's brief was, "Plan well, don't omit a single detail." We must do, "First Time Right!"

The committee had several rounds of discussions with members in different departments during the shift meetings. They invited ideas and identified people who were good at Pookkalam. They made a list of items to be bought. The Pookkalam would begin first thing in the morning. Everyone was asked to be present at the general shift start time. We identified places for making the flower arrangements, which Pookkalam-proficient members would design and execute. Others would help in making available the flowers and other necessary things to avoid waste of time. Some would get engaged in preparing and distributing tea and snacks. Some would just watch and shout motivating words.

The atmosphere was electric, with everyone enthusiastically participating in the Pookkalam. It took more than three hours to make those beautiful flower arrangement designs on the floor. In the end, there were no tired faces; only happy faces with beaming smiles. What a memorable beginning!

The second event of the day was the Onam Sadhya. There was no limit set for the menu. The caterer was asked to include everything that a good Sadhya should consist of. The food was to be served on plantain leaves. There were two types of *'Payasam'* (a desert) in liberal quantities. In other words, the plan looked exciting. After the Pookkalam event, everyone sat for the Sadhya. The first batch took their seats. Others along with the committee members started serving the food. To me, it appeared more like a wedding feast! People serving food encouraged everyone to enjoy their meals. They would watch if any particular item was fully consumed and immediately come with a refill. I loved the Payasam. The moment I gulped it, someone would fill my glass. I must have taken 4–5 glasses. No wonder my blood sugar went up in later years!

The festivities started around 8:00 a.m. and went on till 2:30 p.m. Everyone seemed to enjoy. It was, in fact, a topic for discussion for many days.

Having experienced the power of celebrating Onam together, we knew that this would be one of the mainstays of our culture. In the later years, we made Pookkalam a competition between the four Houses. The real power and attraction of this social function was demonstrated by the celebration we had in the third year.

Few days before Onam that year, when the committee started planning, an issue was flagged off. During the Onam holidays, one of the workers had a wedding in his family. He invited many co-workers. Quite a few planned to attend the wedding. I remember Ravi coming to me for consultation.

"Ghanshyam, we will have a low attendance for Onam celebration this year."

"Why, what happened?"

"One of the workers' sister is getting married on that day. Many workers have decided to attend the wedding."

Now that was a real problem. We discussed for some time and agreed on a way to deal with this problem. Ravi called a meeting of the committee members and discussed a scenario with them.

"What do you do if there is a wedding in your family friend's home?"

"The whole family goes to attend the wedding functions. It's an important function."

"If you and your close family friends have a wedding in your families on the same day, what will you do?"

"Since the wedding is in my family, everybody cannot go. At the same time, we cannot ignore the wedding at my friend's family. So, I will ask someone to go there on behalf of the entire family. Also, we expect someone to come to our function on behalf of that family."

"Onam celebration is like a wedding function for the entire Marico Kanjikode family. But then on the same day, one of our family members has a wedding in his family. What do you think we should do?"

Ravi made a strong point. The committee members understood their responsibility was for both the Kanjikode family and the friend whose sister was getting married. They went back to the people, discussed with the person and others in the shift meetings. They agreed that abstaining from the Onam celebration was against the spirit of Kanjikode culture. So, they agreed that only two to three people would go to the wedding on behalf of the entire Kanjikode team. We heaved a sigh of relief.

On the day of Onam, we found the attendance was thin. Since Pookkalam had become a House competition, I decided to monitor the attendance on a whiteboard right at the entrance of the office building. I wrote the numbers present against each House. A couple of workers got curious.

"What are you writing, sir?"

"These numbers are the number of members present from each House."

"Will this be used for awarding points?"

"Yes, the House with maximum attendance would get extra points."

They quietly left. And then we noticed one person from each House taking his bike and going to town to call all those who were absent. As each person arrived, I kept updating the numbers on the whiteboard. In a short period of time, the attendance went up to almost 95%.

Amazing, I thought! Two key principles were in operation here.

- The power of affiliation: *"My House must not lag behind. We must succeed."*

- The power of Display: *"Everyone is looking at this board. How can we see our performance lower than the other Houses?"*

Apart from a well-planned and executed Onam celebration, we did encourage participating in key functions of our members' families. These social interactions further strengthened the bond.

Teams Involved in Decisions

We strongly practised a culture of inclusion in decision making. Decisions made after consulting with people have a better chance to succeed. In any workplace, there would be new challenges that require a deviation from standards. While we had established standards for carrying out work, there were a few cases which required a different approach. Normally the managers would discuss and prepare a plan, and then ask people to follow the instructions. We tried to involve workers in all critical issues. Let me give you an example.

Due to some reasons, our Mumbai factory had to temporarily stop operations. As a result, we were asked to step up production and dispatch additional supplies to certain markets. Our VP-Operations, Shreekant Gupte, asked us to deploy temporary workers and work in three shifts (instead of the usual two shifts). His idea was to distribute available manpower in three shifts, and give them temporary casual workers to carry out the packaging work. This was clearly against the Kanjikode Vision. We had resolved that we will not have any casual workers. Shreekant and I discussed the dilemma, and then he left the decision to me.

Immediately, the company crisis was shared with the packaging Plant in their shift meeting. Ideas were sought about starting the night shift. The discussions were something like this:

"If we do the packaging in three shifts, we will be able to meet the demand. Otherwise, the company will lose sales, as well as a reputation as a reliable supplier."

"We don't have enough people for three shifts."

"If you agree, we could hire some temporary workers for a few days. Each shift will have a mix of permanent and temporary workers. Critical operation will be done only by our people."

"But, this will be against our Kanjikode Vision. Moreover, the casual workers will have no idea about quality."

"Yes, it will be against the Vision. What do we do then? How do we ensure continuity of supplies?"

The workers animatedly discussed the issue among themselves. They all looked so concerned about the possibility of violation of the 'now sacred' Kanjikode Vision.

"Sir, we will work in two shifts of 12 hours each. This way, we will be able to meet the demand."

"But that would be a violation of not working extra hours. You know that we agreed for NO OVERTIME."

"We will not consider this as overtime work. After the crisis is over, we will take off against extra work without impacting the production."

Now, that was exemplary behaviour. We could see sensitiveness to the company's needs, as well as a strong commitment to the Kanjikode Vision. In my experience, there were not many instances that reflected such mature thinking and passion for the vision. That too in a workforce that was just over two years in this company!

Wage Revisions – Approach Similar to That of Staff

One other area that has the potential to create a wedge between workers and management staff is the approach to annual increments. While for the management staff, there was a structured process for increments based on compensation benchmarking and annual performance appraisal, there was no such process for workers. In all the companies that I had worked with, the workers' wage revision was through a **COD** from the Union. Even in Green Field Projects, Unions would be formed within a year or two, and then they would take help from external trade union leaders to put up the COD and then negotiate. Invariably, that process drained energy and mostly left a bad taste in the mouth.

We decided to do the wage revision proactively. Suraj undertook another study of wage revision in the neighbourhood companies. Both new and older companies were included in this study. Based on this study, wage revision proposal was prepared and circulated among key members of the Top Management team. We had multiple discussions with Jeswant Nair and Shreekant Gupte. After a couple of iterations, the proposal was approved. Wage revision letters were prepared for both skilled and unskilled workers.

Instead of merely handing over the wage revision letters to workers, we decided to do it with some sort of communication in batches. Suraj prepared a presentation and also a set of possible questions with responses. The idea was to ensure uniformity of communication across the masses.

A presentation was made to the workers, explaining the process of benchmarking with neighbouring industries, and the rationale for giving increments to each person. The first reaction was that of delight. They had never expected any increment, never heard from their relatives about such increments within a year of recruitment, and here was their company giving them higher wages! Everyone was happy.

The wage revision process did undergo some improvements in subsequent years, based on raised expectations of the workers as well as the introduction of Workers' Performance Appraisal System.

Peer Rating: Performance Evaluation for Workmen

One of the unique features of the Workers' Performance Appraisal System was 'Peer Rating.' While 70% weightage was given to the Supervisor's rating of the workers' performance and attendance, 30% weightage was given for peers' perception. In essence, each worker was asked to select three peers to rate him on a scale of 10. This was met with some resistance from the supervisors who thought that the peers would be liberal in their rating. However, we convinced them that if we all were living our vision, peers would be realistic in their rating.

After the very first appraisal, the Supervisor of the oil mill came with the peer rating sheet. Each of the three peers had given ten out of ten! The look in his eyes said, *"we told you so!"* We had some discussion about the approach. He went back to his Plant and called the three peers.

"You have given a full rating to this person. Now think about our Kanjikode Vision. Do you think he is perfect and there is no more scope for him to improve?"

"If we think of Kanjikode Vision, he is not perfect. There are areas he can improve."

"So would you like to review your rating?"

They changed their rating to seven out of ten! What the supervisors learnt was that the peers needed to be coached in giving a rating. They also realised that if trusted, the workers could overcome their bias.

All these initiatives together with some others described in later chapters made a huge contribution to building this feeling of **We-ness** among the entire team of Kanjikode. It will not be an exaggeration to say that we set a benchmark for the sense of belongingness.

The House System

One of our dreams was to have the Kanjikode factory without any union. Even though we may have had cordial relations with the trade union leaders, I did not find it palatable that the workers needed external leaders to take care of their interests. They were our members. We should be taking care of them. Why was there a need for them to trust outsiders, rather than the company? In our first interaction with the Attimari Union at the beginning of project work, the trade union leader told me that within a year he would form a union of our workers. My response was if the workers wanted him as their leader, what objection could I have? In my mind, I kept thinking about ways and means to keep away the influence of external leaders.

We identified four essential needs that must be fulfilled if we were to avoid the formation of a Union. The first was to provide an opportunity to lead, the second was a sense of affiliation, the third was a say in welfare activities, and the fourth was a fair wage revision. We were providing opportunities for involvement in various committees (including welfare). The proactive wage revision process was adequately designed and well-accepted. However, we had nothing to fulfil the need for affiliation. Our job rotation plan ensured that workers moved across various roles. They did not belong to one particular Plant. We robbed them of this affiliation to a particular department. This used to trouble me invariably. Also, we needed more avenues for leadership.

One late evening when I reached home, I found my daughter very excited. She wanted to share her happiness with me. So I started talking to her.

"You are very excited today. What happened?"

"Papa, my House won in the basketball game!"

"But, you don't play basketball!"

"I don't, but I belong to the Green House. So, I am very happy!"

How much excitement an affiliation can provide! Even though you are not part of a team, just because you belong to that House is good enough. I carried the thought to work the next day. In our HOD's meeting, I narrated this conversation that I had with my daughter. Why can't we replicate the School House System in our Factory? This will provide everyone with affiliation, and also open opportunities for leading the Houses. The idea struck a positive note. Suraj took up the responsibility of creating a draft note for circulation.

In Marico, we had a very powerful mechanism of testing new ideas in managing people processes across the factories. The MD, VP-HR, VP-Operations, all General Manager Works, HR Managers of Corporate and Works would meet over two days every Quarter. These were well-designed meets. Topics were decided in advance, and designated HR Managers made presentations. This was our lab for testing ideas and making them ready for implementation. We made use of this forum to get inputs for implementation of the House System at Kanjikode. Pankaj Bhargava, then HR Manager of Mumbai Plant, gave many inputs. Finally, the House System was ready.

The key features of the House System were:

- There will be four Houses, each with a distinct name.

- Each House will have a proportionate mix of staff members and workers. Except for the General Manager, everyone else will be part of one or the other House. Allocation of Houses to individuals will be based on a balance of talent.

- Each House will appoint two House Coordinators, one of whom must be from the worker category. Both could be from the workers' category too. The House coordinator's term would be only a year. The idea was to provide leadership opportunity to more and more people through the years.

- Each House will develop an Annual Plan of Action. These could be in the areas of Social Responsibility, such as Health, Education and issues affecting masses. In addition, action plans could include showcasing individual talent in sports and cultural activities.

- The House activities would be closely monitored by the House Coordination Committee consisting of eight House Coordinators (two from each House). The committee will also award points based on various activities and competitions.

- The progress against action plans would be displayed regularly to make everyone aware.

Naming the Houses

To start with, communication was made to all about the House System and its features. A competition was also announced in these meetings for naming the Houses. This was our first action to generate excitement about the initiative. HODs encouraged the workers and the staff members to participate wholeheartedly and win the competition. The response was positive, and the organising committee received a good number of entries.

The next step was to evaluate these entries. Preference was given to names that were well-understood and related to the local culture. The names must sound good, and easy to pronounce. Shortlisted persons were called for a discussion, to understand their rationale for the names. After a lot of deliberation, the entry given by Ravi Nair was selected. He suggested four names associated with music: *Ragam, Thanam, Pallavi and Shruti.*

Allocating Individuals to Houses

Having decided on the House names, the next step was to assign people to Houses. We intended to have a healthy competition between the Houses in various areas. What we did not want was a skew in talent distribution. A balance of talent will make the competition more interesting. Through personal interaction, a complete talent inventory was prepared. The areas of talent included sports, literary interests, music, art, and social inclination. The four HODs were allocated a House each. Other members of the staff and workers were assigned based on the talent inventory.

The allocation was communicated through shift meetings. Now, everyone had an affiliation with a House.

House Coordination Committee

The four Houses had their first meeting to elect the House Coordinators. Each House had a separate session, and the House Members discussed and finalised their Coordinators. By this time, the members already knew which team members had organising capabilities. Only one House chose both Coordinators from the workers' category. The other three Houses had one from staff category as well.

The eight Coordinators formed the House Coordination Committee (HCC). This committee was then asked to meet and plan a set of activities for the year. They then decided to discuss with their House Members and develop a detailed plan. The committee met again to finalise the plan for the year. The first year was the year of learning. The activity list included conducting sports meets, preparing programmes for the annual cultural evening, and interacting with the communities around to provide some helping hand.

It was the responsibility of the HCC to display the plans, monitor the progress and communicate the progress through display boards. They would meet regularly as per the mutually agreed calendar. This review mechanism had a significant role to play in the success of the House System.

Stepping Up the Accelerator

Now that everyone was part of a House and the House Coordinators were performing their roles with enthusiasm, it was time to take the House System to a higher level. We discussed in the Management Team (KMT) meeting to include House Annual Planning as the vital agenda of our Annual Picnic. The Picnic Committee had already done a great job of identifying a beautiful location for our Picnic. Athirappilly Falls in the Thrissur District of Kerala was known for its scenic beauty and plenty of space for activities. After reaching there and soaking in the beauty of the place, we assembled all the members and asked them to do two things in their respective Houses.

The first job of all House Members was to select two Coordinators for the year. Everyone assembled in his/her own House group. I was the only one watching them from a distance. I was enjoying the harmony in the groups as they continued their discussion in a 'Standing Meeting.' They were wearing their T-shirts with the name of the House printed on it (my own T-shirt had the names of all four Houses). The House names, Ragam, Thanam, Pallavi and Shruti, merged so beautifully with the surrounding and the sound of the waterfall. It was sheer music for my ears!

They were quick to decide who would be the two Coordinators for the year. Each House introduced the two new Coordinators to the entire assembly.

The second job they had was to discuss and make a plan for the next year. Each House, led by the two Coordinators, soon finalised what they wanted to do. It was for the Coordinators to share the House Plans. I was amazed by the quality of those action plans. For me, it was all the more gratifying to know that they drew their inspiration from the Kanjikode Vision. Again, this was a true example of a Living Vision! Some of the action plans that remain etched in my mind are given below. I have tried to recollect correctly, the name of the House against each action plan.

- ***We will involve the neighbouring factories in making repairs to the approach road.*** The approach road in the Industrial Area had developed so many huge potholes that the movement of traffic was severely impacted. Though it was the responsibility of KSIDC, there was inadequate action. The Thanam House thought that since this was creating difficulties for everyone, the neighbouring factories would wholeheartedly support them. They would approach them, not as a company, but a House that was sensitive to the needs of people who were working or visiting the factories.

  Post the picnic, the House Coordinators of Thanam House met most of the factory heads in the neighbourhood. Many of them immediately agreed to contribute funds. The House then hired a contractor to fill up the potholes. The speed with which the entire job was done was remarkable. Of course, it was a temporary solution. KSIDC repaired the roads after the monsoon.

  The House drew inspiration from the Kanjikode Vision Pillar, 'External Image.' Other companies well-appreciated the act.

- ***We will visit the local schools and help them overcome some of the difficulties.*** Ragam House too drew inspiration from the Pillar 'External Image.' As a part of this action plan, they visited the primary schools in the area and made a list of their immediate needs.

- ***We will conduct Blood Donation drives.*** Pallavi House ran a blood donation campaign and was able to get many donors. They invited a hospital to set up a blood collection station for a day.

- ***We will improve the implementation of 5S in the Oil Storage Farm.*** Drawing inspiration from the Pillar 'Aesthetics,' the Shruti House decided to work on one of the problem areas of poor housekeeping. Although much work had already been done to stop oil spillage in the tank farm, the look was far from our stated Vision.

The House System was a genuinely empowering initiative. It was path-breaking in the words of Shreekant Gupte, then Vice President Operations. It was an "Innovation in HR" in the words of Harsh Mariwala, then MD and Founder of Marico Innovation Foundation. This was an idea borrowed from schools and implemented with great success in an industrial set up.

To sum up the benefits of the House System:

1. First and foremost it gave a unique identity to people. It helped in strengthening the **We-ness** since House Members belonged to both workers and management categories.

2. It provided leadership opportunities for people. House Coordinators' term of just one year meant more and more would get a chance to become a Coordinator.

3. The fact that more Coordinators were from workers category was a unique experience. Here we had a system where the members included even the HODs, and they were listening to what the leaders were saying. It was a humbling experience that every senior loved!

4. It gave everyone a chance to demonstrate their latent talent. It helped in the overall development of their personalities.

5. It raised the level of Social Responsibility among the members. Organisations generally take the initiative for volunteering in social causes. Here, the efforts were coming from the House Members. The system was creating a high degree of citizenship!

6. The House System was firmly entrenched in the Kanjikode Vision. In fact, our efforts in making the 'Continuous CARE' at the heart of everything that we did were instrumental in the success of the House System.

7. House System became one of the ways to display the progress of initiatives. For example, as stated in the previous chapter, House-wise monitoring of attendance in Onam celebration resulted in very high participation. Another powerful example was improved participation in Kaizen (covered in a later chapter).

Skill Development

The flagship brand of Marico, PCNO, was the market leader. Marico took pride in manufacturing this product with the utmost care and a high focus on quality. It was essential that we train our people extensively so that they could produce high-quality products in the best tradition of Marico.

The Kanjikode Plant had all fresh workers, except for the skilled category who had prior experience. The skilled workers needed to be trained in the specific Plant and Machinery that they were required to operate and maintain. The unskilled category workers had no skills. They were hired for their attitude, and they had a great desire to learn and perform well. It was our responsibility to convert this raw skill into a highly professional workforce.

We had an oil mill that required the workers to work in challenging conditions like higher temperature. Oil mill operation was in three shifts and needed continuous monitoring. It is only through careful monitoring we could produce the Coconut oil of desired quality. The work itself was hard. On the other hand, the packaging Plant had a better environment. This is where PCNO would be filled in primary packs of different sizes and then put in cartons. The process required a focus on the right quantity, absence of any foreign matter in the product, leak-proof sealing, and clean secondary packing (the cartons). Apart from these two Plants, some workers carried out activities like unloading copra bags, copra feeding, handling of packaging materials, and stacking of finished goods.

The one thing we were clear about was that we would not have a separate workforce for the different types of work. We wanted to create a workforce that was skilled in all these types of work. Our focus was on multi-skilling because that would give us a high degree of flexibility in deployment. Since anybody could carry out any work, they could be moved from one work station to another almost immediately. We did not enjoy such flexibility at our other Plants.

Structured Job Rotation

For workers in the unskilled category, we incorporated a very structured Job Rotation Programme. A job rotation schedule was prepared that required every worker to spend a fixed number of days in each of the Plants as well as the stores. The workers used to find the oil mill tenure to be the most difficult one. If there was no rotation, those in the oil mill would have envied the members deployed in other areas. The job rotation created a sense of fairness in their minds.

However, job rotation did have some negative effect. In the beginning, the schedule required a quicker rotation, which did not give enough time for the workers to hone their skills. By the time they became proficient, it was time to move, which resulted in lower productivity and other losses. The rotation design was modified based on this experience. The tenure in each work station was increased, which helped.

At the end of each tenure, the worker's performance was evaluated, which became part of the performance appraisal.

Job rotation helped us to have a flexible workforce. The workers became used to this flexibility, and whenever there was a need to redeploy based on changes in plan, it could be done almost immediately.

Classroom Training

Since seven days of training was factored in manpower planning, we developed a training calendar for classroom training. Apart from skill development training, we had TQM Workshops, Values Workshops and Kanjikode Vision Workshops. All these were conducted in the Conference-cum-Training Hall. Our structured training initiatives ensured that the Hall was almost always booked, and the attendance was full. Most of the trainers were internally developed. For certain types of training, we invited members from other parts of the organisation.

As explained in Creating We-ness chapter, we used classroom training to develop internal trainers. Participants were told that some of them would get the opportunity to play the role of a trainer, based on their interest and performance. This motivated them and made them more focused on learning. The idea of training others appealed to some of them. Later, as trainers, when they faced questions from the participants, they worked even harder to learn. After all, they would not want to be perceived as an ordinary trainer.

Most training modules had a test in the end. Each participant was evaluated based on these tests, as well as the level of participation during the training. Feedback was taken from the participants at the end of the training program. In addition, the usefulness of the training program was evaluated based on feedback taken from the respective Head of Departments, a week after the training. These feedbacks were used for making necessary improvements in the training modules.

Involvement in Making Standard Operating Procedures and Work Instructions

Our operating teams had already made various procedures and work instructions with the help of the Corporate Quality Team and other operating Plants. The operating executives were well-versed and ensured that the members followed these procedures. Over time we realised the need for ownership of these written documents at the grassroots level. A team of executives and workers was formed to rewrite the Operating Procedures and Work Instructions. The idea was to encourage them to write exactly what was being practised. In the process, the documents became more user-friendly. The team took inputs from other members of the operating teams. The involvement of workers made them feel proud and helped create a sense of ownership. They were more aware of the need to improve, whenever a problem arose.

Jobs Enriched with Passage of Time

In the beginning, everyone was trying hard to follow the instructions and produce quality work. Slowly, the members became proficient in their work. They would ask questions to understand the logic of doing things, the reasons for certain specific requirements, and so on. This was an indicator of the success of our Recruitment Process, Training Process and member engagement initiatives. Our members were intelligent and showed interest in learning. Some of them started asking for the inclusion of activities that would make their job more exciting and more enriched. Coming from them, it was a welcome idea. We had an internal discussion, and then took inputs from Corporate Quality Assurance. Some of the initiatives we implemented were:

1. **Packaging Material Inspection:** The workers in the packaging material section were initially entrusted with the tasks of unloading, counting, stacking and issuing the packing materials in the warehouse. The Quality Supervisor typically did the packaging material inspection. Some of these quality inspections were delegated to the workers, who proudly took up the responsibility. The role of the Quality Supervisor changed from Inspector to Trainer and Auditor.

2. **Data Logging:** A job that was done by the supervisors was entrusted to some workers. The onus was on the supervisors to train the workers, and ensure error-free work.

Communication

Communication is one of the critical factors in the success of any organisation. The Leadership at Marico had realised this early, and that was one reason why the company succeeded in creating an open culture, even though most of the senior and middle-level managers were from companies with distinct management styles. At Kanjikode, we not only followed the well-tested company practices but also adopted some of the best practices of other organisations.

Organisation Communication Exercise (OCE)

The annual OCE was held at the Corporate Office, all production facilities, and the four sales regions. It was an opportunity for all employees to interact with their Top Management directly. It was a day-long exercise, where the Top Management team and the local Management Team made the presentation. These were followed by an Open House—a question and answer session. The annual exercise focused on the dissemination of information on results of the past year, as well as the plans for the next year. Some of the presentations by the local teams would be about the challenges, and how those could be addressed. Everyone looked forward to the OCE. Undoubtedly, this was the most awaited event of the year.

The first OCE in Kanjikode Works was held in the packaging Plant. The biggest challenge in designing the OCE was the language. The presentations were typically in English, and here we had our masses, who hardly understood the language. To ensure the effectiveness of the OCE, it was essential that the questions were answered in Malayalam. Our Vice President HR, Jeswant Nair, took it upon himself to do this. Any questions on local issues were to be responded by the local team. Everyone was full of enthusiasm. For the workers, it was unique. Many had spoken to their relatives about this event, and they learnt that such things did not happen in other local companies.

Everyone assembled at the venue well before the time. As they were seated, the first thing I noticed was the tendency to sit in groups, which was so evident by the different uniforms. The supervisory staff in their light-coloured uniform were very conspicuous. I made a mental note of that and decided to address it as soon as possible after the OCE. A sense of anticipation was in the air. After all, it was their first full-day interaction with the Top Management.

As the presentation progressed, Jeswant would explain in Malayalam where needed. Later, during the question and answer session, some questions were answered by Suraj. It was all going well until someone asked one question that almost created a pin-drop silence. The question was unanticipated and took everyone by surprise.

A worker asked smiling, *"Many of us work after office hours, yet we don't get any overtime. Isn't it unfair?"* Suraj translated that question in English.

Obviously, this had to be answered. Despite my inability to speak in Malayalam, I stood up and asked, *"Do you remember the Kanjikode Vision?"*

A resounding "Yes" was the collective response.

"What does it say?"

"We would like to build a factory..." I clapped and stopped them.

"What does it say about working hours and overtime?"

"That we will avoid working beyond the work hours."

"Yes, we don't want to invite the disease of overtime. But, we also want to create a model factory. In the beginning, we all had to work harder and

much beyond the work hours. By now, the number of instances of working beyond shift hours has come down. Do you agree that we have been able to do this?" (Suraj helped in translating this in Malayalam for wider understanding).

"Yes, earlier we worked much more."

"This is all because of our Kanjikode Vision. Do you believe that one day we will be able to completely remove the instances of working overtime? Are we working in that direction?"

"Yes, we can do that."

"So, where is the problem? Let us clap for our Kanjikode Vision."

Everyone stood up and clapped happily.

I strongly believe that the above interaction helped some of the non-believers to have faith in the power of a well-shared vision. I am glad this conversation happened that day, for it reinforced my own faith. Through strict monitoring by the KMT, we were able to achieve the 'No Overtime' goal!

Overall, the first OCE was a great success. Our staff and workers talked about it among themselves and with their friends and relatives, which further strengthened 'External Image,' one of the five Pillars of Kanjikode Vision.

Shift Meetings

Shift Meetings were essentially a work planning and delegation meeting. It was a brief meeting held by the shift Supervisor with his team. Typically, it was a standing meeting, where he would explain the work plan for the shift and allocation of duties to each individual. These were the normal shift meetings, but when required, special shift meetings were held where some key communications were made to the workforce. Such special meetings would be addressed by the Departmental Head and HR Head, as required. Special shift meetings ensured timely and speedy communication of important issues to the entire workforce, thus eliminating any hearsay and gossip. Shift meetings were also used as a platform by improvement project teams seeking inputs, Canteen Committee taking feedback on canteen issues, etc.

Weekly Departmental Meetings

Each Head of Department was required to have a meeting with his team, every week. In these meetings, work-related issues would be discussed. Supervisors were encouraged to come up with ideas to improve work methods. Any grievances would be addressed and resolved by the team. Any unresolved issues would be promptly escalated for resolution. The HOD would invite other HODs depending on need. For example, if there was any issue related to Warehousing and Materials, the Commercial Manager would attend the Departmental Meeting of the Production Manager. For any people-related and administrative issues, the HR Manager would attend the meetings. These meetings helped in dealing with the situation in time.

Once a month, I would attend the departmental meetings to get a flavour of its proceedings. My presence reinforced the impression that the Unit Head was easily accessible.

Management by Walking Around (MBWA)

The one practice we had established early was that every member of the KMT, that is all the Departmental Heads and me, would take rounds of the facility in the morning. It was not only for monitoring the work progress but also to meet and talk to people. I think MBWA provided an excellent opportunity for informal communication, gauging the mood of people, and giving on the spot appreciation as well as any corrective feedback. Personally, the MBWA brought me closer to the people. I used it for reinforcing the Kanjikode Vision.

Despite our language barrier, the workers would talk to me about new improvements they made, any new achievements in their work or House activities, how they reinforced a particular Pillar of the Kanjikode Vision, etc. I asked simple questions that they could easily understand, and could tell me simply or show what they did. So easy was the communication, that I never felt the need to really learn Malayalam!

Once, a worker in the packaging Plant came forward to show me his Kaizen. *"Sir, I have done a Kaizen."*

"What is it about? Show me."

He took me to the filling line where the 200 ml tins were being filled up. He showed me a small air tube fitted at the entry point of the conveyor where the empty tins were getting loaded.

"Sir, we found that some loose cardboard particles were stuck in the empty tins. This could lead to a potential complaint from the market. The air from this tube directly hits the inside of each tin. Since these are light particles, the air flushes them out. So, we will never have any complaint of this type."

I was impressed and patted him. I also called the Plant Supervisor and other workers and appreciated his Kaizen then and there. He felt so proud when we all appreciated his Kaizen. A broad smile on his face! These public appreciations rubbed off on others.

Open Door Policy

We knew that it was essential to be highly accessible, available for any consultation, and ready to resolve issues speedily. Open Door Policy was practised by Marico at all locations, and we too had adopted it. Except when any meeting was going on inside, we used to keep our glass doors open. This encouraged anyone to just come in if they wanted to talk. The design of the office with glass partitions and open work stations conveyed a sense of openness.

In the early days, I would come out of my cabin if I spotted any worker visiting the administration building, and bring him along to my cabin to have an informal chat. Others noticed, and gradually the number of members visiting my cabin increased. Our discussion used to be centred on their learning, working environment, Kanjikode Vision, and at times their personal lives. These interactions strengthened our bonding as a Team.

These various approaches to two-way communication went a long way to building trust. The message was loud and clear. Here was a management that was always accessible and willing to deal with any issues without losing time. Here was an organisation that cared for us. All that was needed was to approach and talk.

We were also aware of the possibility of a communication gap. So we educated the entire management staff about the need for identifying such issues and quickly escalating for immediate resolution. Here is an example of how swiftly we dealt with a miscommunication.

As I was sitting in my cabin, I got a call from the Packaging Plant Supervisor. *"Sir what did you tell the two boys who came to the administration building to get some supplies?"*

I recalled. Every shift, two workers used to come to the pantry to take the supplies for making tea in their Plant. That afternoon, I met them at the pantry. I saw their hands were soiled. Smilingly, I told them to be careful so that the white walls do not get stained if they put their hands there. It seemed to be a harmless conversation. But apparently, they misunderstood. They thought they were being admonished.

When I told the Supervisor about the interaction, he said, *"Sir, can you please come here immediately? There is a huge misunderstanding."* Without losing time, I went straight to the Plant.

I smiled at the gathering. They smiled back. I asked, *"What happened?"* The Supervisor said, *"The boys thought you were admonishing them. They don't want to go to the pantry again."*

I asked the two boys to narrate the incident again to all and asked the Supervisor to interpret in English. During this, I asked him to ask the boys what would have happened if they had touched the walls by mistake. The boys said, *"It would have soiled."*

"How would the office look if the walls were soiled?"

"It would look dirty."

"Would it have been in line with the Kanjikode Vision? Which Pillars would have been impacted?" This question was for everybody.

"Aesthetics and External Image," was the answer.

I asked, *"Why External Image?"*

"Outsiders come to the administration building, and they would carry a bad image if the office looked dirty."

So now the discussion went to the Kanjikode Vision. They agreed that before entering the office area, they would ensure that their hands are not soiled. We all had our tea together in the Plant. A potential conflict had been nipped in the bud. I congratulated the Supervisor for immediately calling me, and thanked everyone for a good discussion on Kanjikode Vision.

Using the Community to Deal with Indiscipline

The genesis of this unique initiative lies with the issue of indiscipline related to attendance. While the Model Code of Conduct had a defined approach for dealing with indiscipline, we wanted a more effective method to deal with such situations. There were a couple of cases of absenteeism that needed to be taken up for resolution. Absenteeism disturbed the smooth functioning of teams and negatively impacted performance. In our opinion, it was not a matter to be resolved by the Management Team alone. Since teams are affected, they should be part of the solution.

With this in mind, we started discussing the ways and means to involve the entire team. Our discussion slowly veered to olden times when the whole village used to participate in dealing with aberrant behaviour of certain individuals. The involvement of the entire community put so much pressure on the individual that he would have no option but to improve. Moreover, if the behaviour did not improve, the community would take a collective decision to excommunicate him. In Hindi, we call it, *"Hukka Pani band karna!"* While the village elders took the decision, it was supported by the whole community.

The HOD Team decided to take up the case of one worker, who was invariably absenting himself. He was called to explain his conduct. He said he had some personal problems, but he would improve. Initially, he did, but soon he started missing work again. Through family involvement, he was called to appear before the team. This time the team took a stern approach. He proposed that if he missed work on a particular day, he would compensate it by working extra hours on subsequent days. The HOD Team decided to involve the entire Production Team. He reiterated his proposal to his entire team.

"If I am absent any day, I will compensate by working extra hours on subsequent days."

The team said, *"It's not an acceptable proposal."*

"But why? I will be working the required number of hours!"

"We work as a team. When one person does not come, it affects the performance. Even if we manage that day, how are your extra hours going to help? The team is not going to get any benefit."

It was a very mature assessment that came from the workers. The HODs were very impressed with their response. They asked, *"What should be an acceptable proposal?"*

"We should give him fixed time to improve. If he does not improve, he should agree to resign, so that another deserving person can be recruited. We should not waste our time in hearing his stories again. He has been given enough chances. Let him give an undated resignation letter, which will be accepted the moment he breaks his promise."

Indeed, the community was very strict. I must say, they were stricter than the Management Team itself. So, an undated letter was signed by the worker. Not much later, the boy broke his promise and was relieved from employment based on his resignation letter.

This case was a success story of peoples' involvement in critical decision making. It only helped us to fine-tune the process for the future. It was time for The Jury System to take birth, which happened under the overall leadership of Vijayan, my successor. The HR Manager, Salil Raghavan, worked on the process.

A team consisting of managers, supervisors and workers were tasked with the job of defining the role and process for dealing with the case. This team was called the Jury. In the first meeting, the Jury elected Raju Sekhar, Production Executive, as its leader. The Jury was defined as follows:

"A representative body of the community to analyse and evaluate critical issues like chronic absenteeism and recommend suitable action to the community. The decision to form a Jury should be derived out of the community, sensing the importance of such issues."

"The Jury can recommend norms if similar cases happen again in the future. The Jury will maintain ongoing communication with the rest of the community through Shift Meetings."

"Community whetting of the Jury recommendations is essential for final action."

The first case was taken up by this Jury. Following were some of the observations made by the Jury members:

1. As per the records, this worker had given many commitments to improve, but he never met them.
2. His quality of work was poor.
3. He was not given adequate chances to improve (as perceived by some Jury members).

The Jury decided to go to the community through Shift Meetings, and take the mass view about giving him a hearing by the Jury. The general view that emerged was to give him a hearing. Two days later he was called for a hearing.

In the second meeting of the Jury, the worker was asked to explain his conduct and the reasons for his errant behaviour. His reasons included post-marriage issues and poor health of his grandfather.

He agreed to be regular, but the Jury was not convinced. Some Jury members were seeking his separation, while some wanted to give him yet another chance. After a heated discussion, the Jury decided to punish him, but also give him a chance.

"We will ask him to resign. And then he should apply again, and start afresh as a Trainee."

The Jury also decided to send a small team to his House to verify his claims of his personal problems. Post the visit, the team found that the real cause of his absenteeism was alcoholism and bad company. The grandparents thought he might improve if he changed the location of his residence.

In the next meeting, the Jury decided to give a chance with the following conditions:

1. He should resign from the company with effect from the date his chronic absenteeism started. That was over four months earlier.
2. He should shift to Kanjikode with his wife, so that he would remain under the focus of community members, and therefore will have better control over his drinking.
3. If he agreed to the above, he could reapply as a Trainee.

The Jury thought that the Training Stipend might not be enough to support himself as well as his wife. They recommended that his wife should be helped to find employment with help from the company if a request was made.

The next step was to seek the community's approval. The Jury communicated the recommendations to the community through the Shift Meetings. The decisions were highly appreciated.

The errant employee was called by the Jury and was informed about the community decision. He was clearly told that the chance was being given to him out of compassion for his family. He accepted all the conditions and submitted his pre-dated resignation.

This entire case was resolved within seven days. It not only made the Jury members happy but also established faith among the community members about the fairness of the process.

So strong was the message that after this case, the remaining 2/3 cases of chronic absenteeism were desperate to discuss their improvement plans with their HOD and the HR Head.

Involvement

In the chapters so far, the involvement of people is a common thread across all the initiatives. It is because we started our work with the principle of involvement. Right from the beginning, we were looking for opportunities for involving the masses. We believed that involvement leads to shared ownership, which leads to superior results. In this chapter, I would like to describe some of the other key initiatives that show the level of involvement achieved at Kanjikode.

Kaizens

Marico had embarked on a journey of TQM. With the help of our TQM Consultants, implementation was started at Kanjikode as well. One of the key initiatives in this journey was Kaizen (small improvements). The idea was to encourage individuals and teams to come up with ideas that will lead to improvement of the product, quality, productivity, cost, safety and morale of people.

There is always a debate on what kind of improvement will be recorded as a Kaizen. In some places, there is a tendency to question a recorded Kaizen. As a result, people get confused and shy away from recording due to the fear of ridicule. This defeats the purpose of Kaizen. We believed that Kaizen is a way of encouraging the creativity of people and ensuring mass participation. So, we made the following rules:

1. Any improvement, small or big, will qualify for a Kaizen if there is a clear difference between 'Before' and 'After' situations.

2. A Kaizen can be reported only after it has been implemented. If the idea generator does not have the means to implement, he/she could take help from those who could do the implementation. In that case, both will get the credit for the Kaizen.

3. The Kaizen form would be filled up showing the nature of improvement and the benefits from it.

We realised that our factory had immense opportunities for making hundreds of small improvements. So, we said that we should be able to get more than two improvements per person per month. We had learnt that some companies in Japan (the birthplace of the Kaizen concept) had these kinds of targets.

As we began training people in Kaizen, many got enthused by the idea. They only needed to be encouraged and helped. Above all, it required continuous monitoring. All departments took the same target, and the HODs started monitoring the progress daily. Our TQM Coordinator came with the idea of a 'Daily Score' and the 'Asking Rate.' The pace was slowly picking up.

We decided to give more visibility to the progress of Kaizens. Notice boards at various places started tracking the progress. The key indicators were:

- Current Kaizen per person
- Asking rate per person
- Participation rate (percentage of departmental people reporting Kaizens)

All these were ranked department-wise as well, which showed the best performing and the worst performing departments. Visibility led to healthy competition. No department wanted to be left behind. Every month, all the Kaizen contributors were given prizes. More than the token prize, the individuals used to feel the pride of having contributed.

We had a whiteboard at the entrance of the office. Every morning, I would spend some time in front of the board, and write my remarks on the Kaizen Scorecard. I would speak to the departmental employees with lower scores and ask them what they intended to do to reach their target. I used to pat those who were doing well. In my Plant rounds, I would ask supervisors and workers about their Kaizens and go deeper into what they did, how they did it, and what benefits were achieved. These small steps helped. They say, *"What Gets Reviewed, Gets Improved."*

Soon, Kanjikode became the leading contributor of Kaizens among all locations in Marico. The enthusiasm level of the people at Kanjikode had gone up so high that they started achieving higher and higher targets. The average Kaizens per person per month went up to a dizzy level of 5.6! The quality of some of the Kaizens showed how seriously our members were involved. A couple of examples are:

- Improvement of boiler fuel efficiency, which was accepted and recognised by the manufacturer.

- Installing a flexible compressed air line on the Filling Machine, to ensure that there was no ingress of loose particles in the packed tin.

The employee involvement levels due to the TQM initiatives had touched a high standard. There were reports that many were implementing some of these concepts in their personal lives. I had a chance to witness one such case. During one of my Plant rounds, one of the oil mill members, Babu, told me that he had implemented the housekeeping principles at his home.

I asked him, *"What exactly have you done?"*

"Sir, please visit my home. You can see for yourself."

He knew that I passed by his village on my way home.

"My shift ends at 2 p.m. I will wait till the evening, and accompany you when you are ready to leave."

I thought about it and then agreed to visit his home the next day. He introduced me to his parents, and then proudly showed me around. It was a very neat and clean house. There was a good use of signage that gave a unique appearance to his house. I was really happy to see this level of involvement. The next day I shared my experience with all the employees during my Plant round. Babu was very happy to get public recognition.

Various Committees

While the Kaizen initiative gave individuals a chance to improve their work-related situations as well as an opportunity to express their creative side, membership to multiple committees allowed them to develop their leadership and team skills. Nomination to a committee was considered prestigious. To ensure that more and more people got this opportunity, the membership was rotated at fixed intervals.

The most important committee was the HCC, which had a variety of roles throughout the year. This has already been described in the chapter on House System. Only one more thing I would like to say about this committee is that it did a great job in ensuring that the projects across the four Houses did not clash with each other. So, if a House takes a community project in the area of health, others would not take it. They truly believed that together, all of them had a lot of areas to focus on.

The other committee that did a great job was the Canteen Committee. It is not easy to build a consensus on the canteen menu. Yet, this committee would discuss alternatives, go back to people, talk to them, and finally come up with a decision that was accepted by all. In addition to this job, the committee also had to manage printing, issuing and accounting of coupons. But they liked it. It gave them something different to do.

Customer Visits

The core job of our members was to produce quality products to meet customer requirement. We thought it was important to expose them to external customers. In the customer chain, we had the Distributors and the Retailers who finally sold the products to the ultimate consumers. With the help of the Regional Sales team, we organised **customer visits** for our supervisors and workers. It was to be a day-long visit where a group of 10–12, accompanied by the Area Salesperson, would first visit the Distributor and then the Retailer. The next morning, the group would make a presentation of their experience and findings.

This gave them a good idea of how their own output affected the customers. They would come up with suggestions that would help improve the perception of these primary customers. One group narrated the following experience at a Retailer's shop.

Retailer: *"Sometimes we get different shades of cartons. Why don't you supply the same shade every time?"*

Group: *"The carton is only meant to safely transport the packs. How does the difference in shade matter?"*

Retailer: *"I agree that it is for the safety of packs. But, the difference in shade puts doubt in our minds about the genuineness of the supply."*

The group was convinced that it was a genuine concern. Our product being a **market leader,** many spurious stocks were making rounds in the market place. This issue was subsequently escalated, and action was taken to correct the situation.

Participation in Small Group Activities

As part of our TQM Journey, we adopted Small Group Activity (SGA). This was basically a structured problem-solving methodology where teams worked on their chronic problems. There were various teams consisting of the staff and the workers. They were trained in the Structured Problem-Solving Methodology and the Seven Quality Tools. The teams had structured meetings at fixed intervals. They became adept in data collection and then used the tools to analyse the data systematically.

Whenever a team needed to take input from others, they would do that in the Shift Meetings. They would first explain their findings and then ask for input. I still remember one particular case, which I thought was very powerful. A team was working on a problem in the oil mill. While on the diagnostic journey, they identified various potential causes and prepared a cause and effect diagram. They then posted it on the oil mill display board and explained the diagram to all the members of 'B' Shift. They asked them to mark on the chart if they had any specific comments, including anything that needed to be added, removed, or modified.

They then requested the 'B' Shift Supervisor to explain the same to the people in the 'C' Shift. The same was expected from the 'A' shift next morning. The team gave the shifts 24 hours to add, delete, and modify the chart. When they came back the next day, they were happy to see various inputs marked in different colours.

So, if a small team worked on a problem, they ensured that all concerned were involved. It will not be an exaggeration to say that everyone was comfortable in involving others. There was no hesitation in seeking ideas from anyone at any level.

Presentations to Visitors

The new Marico Plant attracted visitors from all parts of the organisation. There was always a constant stream of visitors. At times, there would be a large group. The largest was the Sales and Marketing team from Corporate and Regions. Also, the word about our unique culture and practices had spread all around. We received requests from other companies for a visit to have a firsthand experience of what we were doing.

Our workers were involved in telling visitors about our practices. They would accompany them around the Plant and tell them about the products, process and facets of our culture. This further strengthened the sense of belongingness among our workforce. They proudly participated in such activities. The visitors, invariably, were impressed by the workers who spoke about the company, their vision and their culture. Not only did the visitors give positive feedback, but they also helped in the word-of-mouth publicity of our unique culture.

Certainly, we were moving to achieve the Kanjikode Vision, "We would like to build a factory…a prototype within Marico and Kerala."

Attimaris: From Adversaries to Associates

Earlier in the book, I wrote about the 'Initial Setback' caused by the conflict with the Attimaris. Whatever the initial experience, and whatever the image this group of people had in Kerala, we decided to do something that helped them see themselves as our associates. After all, they were providing us with an important service throughout the day. They were always focused on their work, and never tried to create any fuss as long as we stayed within the contractual norms. That worked fine with us. The first opportunity to involve them beyond the work came during the first Onam celebrations.

One of the most important parts of the Onam celebrations, was the Onam Sadhya, a community feast. Apart from our employees, we decided to invite our business associates. Ravi, our Commercial Manager, came to me and said, *"We are inviting our Contractors and Vendors for the Sadhya. Should we also invite the Attimaris?"*

So far, we had never really considered them as our associates. They were not the usual socially bonding types. They would only enter the premises to work. All conversations were related to just the work. We thought it was a good idea to invite them. We were not sure if they would come.

After some discussions, we decided to extend an invitation to them. To our surprise, they accepted our invitation. This was their first social interaction with the company. We continued to invite them in the future as well. This initiative was the first step into turning them into real associates. The following examples remain etched in my memory.

There was a situation in late 1995 when production at our Mumbai factory had to be stopped briefly. As a result, the Kanjikode factory was asked to make some urgent supplies to the market. It was late afternoon when the instructions came. The supplies had to reach the market the next morning. What it meant was that the trucks would have to be loaded and dispatched late in the evening. As per our contract with the Attimaris, there would be no loading or unloading operation after 5 p.m. Sreekumaran, our Dispatch Supervisor came to my cabin, and said, *"Sir, empty trucks can be arranged only around 5 p.m. The Attimaris will not agree to load. We cannot dispatch the products today. Please speak to the Head Office."*

I asked him to try reasoning with the Attimari leader. *"Tell him the situation. Tell him that if we don't supply, our image in the market will be impacted. Tell him that as per contract he is not bound to do the loading. Ask him what should be done in such a case. In no case should you request to load the truck."*

He went back to engage the Attimari leader. Almost an hour passed, and I did not hear from him. I was concerned. I left a message in his office to immediately call me. Five minutes later, I got his call. His voice was excited, and he narrated to me.

"Sir, as you suggested I spoke to the leader. Initially, he was angry. Then he said since it was the matter of company image, he would ask his team to stay back and load the truck. He asked me to get the truck immediately. Since I was arranging for the truck, I could not call you. Now the loading has just started."

"There is one more thing sir! He said that we should tell the Head Office not to ask us for such urgent dispatches. They will not help the next time."

That was something! Totally unexpected from a community that never worked beyond rules! On one side he agreed to help, and at the same time cautioned how important it was for them to stick to their rules. The fact that the leader spoke about company image made us very happy. Now, these guys too were developing a feeling of ownership for the company.

The other instance took place a couple of months later. The oil mill had a by-product called copra cake. While the oil was further processed and packed as finished goods, the cake was filled up in bags and then sold to third parties. Loading of these bags was part of the job done by the Attimaris. All dispatches took place on weekdays. There was no loading and dispatch on Sundays.

A situation arose whereby it was necessary to operate the oil mill on a Sunday. There was not enough space to stack the cake bags inside the Plant. If the Plant had to run, at least some of the cake bags must be dispatched. We asked Sreekumaran, our Dispatch Supervisor to approach the Attimari leader, explain the actual situation to him, and seek his advice. He had a positive experience the last time. He was somewhat optimistic. However, his apprehension was that the whole group stayed far off, and coming on a Sunday may not appeal to them.

The Attimari leader listened to him and understood the situation. He asked, *"What is the minimum number of trucks that will create enough space for the mill to continue running?"*

"Four."

"We will deploy a team for loading these trucks tomorrow morning. You run your mill, and the balance material will be loaded on Monday morning. We don't want to call everyone for the whole day on a Sunday."

"That will be sufficient."

The next day, trucks were placed and loaded as planned. Thanks to their cooperation, the oil mill could run without any space constraint.

Our positive approach did make inroads in the hearts of the Attimaris, and we could now consider them our associates.

Achievements

This story about Kanjikode Works of Marico started with the intention of putting all the learning of the organisation together to create a truly empowering culture. It was possible, because not only the local team but everyone else in Marico who could contribute, did contribute. It was possible because we were always thinking of something different that will produce better results. It was possible because the Top Management under the leadership of Harsh Mariwala was backing us.

So, what were the achievements that made every one of us feel proud? There were many.

High External Image

One of the Pillars of the Kanjikode Vision was 'External Image.' While Marico was known in the industry for being a responsible corporate citizen, in Kerala, we were known more as a major buyer of copra. We enjoyed a good image in certain business circles. What we wanted was to have a distinct image in public, specifically in Kerala.

Setting up a factory requires getting many approvals and certifications from Statutory Authorities. In those days, it was not so easy. We went about establishing a rapport with such authorities. We wanted to stress upon our desire to follow all the rules and be known as a responsible corporate citizen. My job required me to meet the Ministers, Secretaries and Key Officers of various Departments in the State Government of Kerala. At every opportunity, I spoke about our company, and what we stood for. I shared our vision for the Kanjikode factory. I spoke about our high standards of recruitment and skill development. I shared our dream of creating a **model factory** in Kerala. These had the desired effects. Slowly, in the Government circles, we started getting the recognition.

We had been promised certain benefits for setting up a factory in Kerala. However, this required the Government to pass an Order. It required several representations and meetings with the Government to finally make them pass the GO. But, at the last stage, we found that the file was stuck somewhere. So far, I was handling all liaisons directly. At this stage, I decided to send one of our officers, Suresh, to meet the departmental clerks and find out the problem. He was clearly told to talk about his company, how it was different, and what good work it was doing in Kerala. He followed the instructions to the tee.

His experience was so positive that when he returned, we could all see his sense of achievement. He got a good response, and the clerks ensured that the file was moved. After one more such visit, the GO was passed, and we were able to get the benefits we were promised.

Another example of a good 'External Image' was related to our interaction with the Factories and Boiler Inspector. In the very beginning, we explained to the Inspector that we would not flout any rules. In fact, we would do much more than what the statute desired. He was very sceptical. He said that he would be very strict if we were found to violate any rules. Some people told us that he was a difficult person, and would create a lot of obstacles.

As a part of his job, he would make factory visits. Every time he came, I (along with Suraj, our HR Head) would accompany him to the factory and make notes of his observations. Then we would have discussions in my cabin about steps to be taken. Over a period of time, six months perhaps, he became convinced about our commitment to the rules. In his subsequent visits, he would meet me in the beginning, then go for factory rounds with Suraj, and again meet me before leaving. That was a big change. At last, our efforts were succeeding.

As time passed, other Industries started interacting with us. They wanted to learn from us. We had arrived!

Award from Kerala Productivity Council

Our good work was getting noticed. Our employees, our business associates and our friends, talked about our unique ways of managing a factory. The interaction of our officers at various Professional Bodies gave others insight into our methods. The Kerala Productivity Council visited our facility to study the warehousing practices. They were surveying several factories to understand how these practices differed from each other.

Some days later, we were told that our factory would be given an award for most innovative warehousing practices. The Commercial Team, in particular, was very happy at this recognition. We all rejoiced in their celebration.

Best Factory Award in Marico

Marico had a good practice of holding the Annual Operations Meet. One of the agendas of this meet was to recognise Factories, Departments and Individuals in various areas. We had already been recognised for Best TQM Implementation and Innovative HR Practices. The ultimate achievement was when the Kanjikode Factory received the 'Best Factory Award' in 1995–96. The Kanjikode Vision mentions, "…building a factory and organisation…as a prototype within Marico…"

National HR Excellence Award from National HRD Network

A National-level HR Excellence Contest was held by the National HRD Network (Delhi Chapter) and Amity Business School, Delhi. The Contest was focused on Innovative HR Practices in Indian Organisations.

Out of a total of about 160 Organisations who took part in the Contest, nine were shortlisted to make the final presentation at Amity Business School Auditorium in July 1997. My successor, P. Vijayan made the presentation along with Pankaj Bhargava (Corporate HR) and Salil Raghavan (Kanjikode HR).

The Jury was unanimous in their selection of the winner. It was Marico, Kanjikode Works. The other worthy winners were C-Dot and Bharat Shell (for Second Prize), and Core Health Care, J.K. Corporation and HCL-HP (for the Third Prize).

Such recognitions speak a lot about the efforts and the results achieved. This particular recognition went beyond the Kanjikode Vision, which talked about achievement in Marico and Kerala. Here was recognition at the National level. Extremely gratifying!

No Union for Six Years

At the end of our first interaction with the trade union leader about the Attimari demand, he had said, *"I will be forming a Union in your factory within a year."*

My response to him was, *"If our workers choose you as their leader, you will be most welcome. But I don't think there will be such a need."*

After that, we went about building our culture brick by brick. We got too busy ensuring continuous communication, people development and involvement in endless activities and creating a large family where every member cared for each other. We created a high sense of belongingness and ownership. We proactively gave them increments without anyone asking for it, and we even started an Appraisal Process to reward workers based on performance.

Coming back to the BMS trade union leader, I did not hear from him or see him for the next two years. And then he met me one day to convey his condolence over the tragic death of our HR Head, Suraj.

We were all assembled at the Hospital in Palakkad, where the bodies of two of our most valuable people were to be handed over to us. Suraj and Hari drowned in a lake a day earlier, where they had gone for a picnic. Their bodies were recovered in the morning. It was a big shock to everyone. The BMS leader spoke highly of Suraj.

The union leader did not have much interaction with Suraj but had kept track of what was going on in our factory. *"You remember I told you that I would form a Union within a year?"*

"Yes, of course, I remember. What happened?"

"I keep hearing about the work you guys are doing for the development and welfare of the workers. I don't think we could have done so much if we had our Union. Our purpose is not to disturb if things are going well."

The statement coming out from a trade union leader meant a lot. I thanked him.

The Kanjikode factory continued to work without the formation of any union for six years. That was truly remarkable for a State like Kerala, which was known for multiple unions in almost every organisation.

Final Words

Having written about my experience, I am feeling a sense of relief. Almost everything mentioned in this book is over two decades old. But, it feels as if everything happened recently. The feeling of relief is because I have finally documented what many wanted me to do all along. This book is a tribute to all those who made it possible—the organisational leadership, the other factories, the support departments, our business associates, and all the members of the Kanjikode team.

If we succeeded, it was because of the transparent approach, something we learnt from our corporate culture. At the outset, we told ourselves that if Marico prided itself with an enabling **work culture,** we should be able to succeed in creating an empowered organisation even in a place like Kerala and we surpassed our own expectations.

At the corporate level, we had a team that walked the talk. At Kanjikode, we created a team that followed these footsteps. Every leader was committed and led his team from the front. So, if it was a Kaizen target, the Departmental Heads and the Section Executives would meet their individual goals so that others would get inspired.

We took up a large number of initiatives. We succeeded in each of those because we spent hours on detailed planning, ensured everyone worked hard and monitored the progress frequently. We celebrated every little success and took corrective actions in a timely manner.

We knew that any change at the top level would have to be handled well to ensure continuity. So, when it was time to hand over the reins to Vijayan, we took a couple of steps. The first step was to have a team exercise just before the change. The KMT Members had a two-day workshop to discuss possible impacts of change, and develop a plan to deal with situations that may arise. The brainstorming session was very intense. The team considered several possible scenarios. The one standard resolution was that every issue should be aligned to the Kanjikode Vision. So, if there was any conflicting view, it should be discussed with the new leader with reference to the five Pillars of Kanjikode Vision.

The other thing we did was to make a symbolic handover of the Kanjikode Vision in front of the entire workforce in the canteen. It helped in reinforcing our belief that the Kanjikode Vision was paramount, and served as a beacon to run the organisation. On his part, Vijayan not only played a great role in living the vision but also involved everyone to review the vision to make any changes. That was a wonderful step he took three years after taking charge of the factory.

Coming Back for Real-Time Strategic Change

The Kanjikode experience was my most valued experience. It helped me evolve as a person and as a leader. I felt very close to all the members of the Kanjikode team, as well as the external people associated with us. In due course of time, I left Marico, and then subsequently became an independent Management Consultant. In the summer of 2002, I got a call from Rakesh Pandey, the then Chief Human Resource Officer. Rakesh was earlier part of our Operations Team, as General Manager of the Mumbai factory. He asked me if I could do an intervention at the Kanjikode Factory. That excited me. Going back to Kanjikode, engaging with the people there, and helping them with their issues would be worthwhile.

I had a meeting with Vasan, the Manufacturing Head. He discussed the situation and the issues that were impacting the performance of the unit. I suggested the use of Large Scale Interactive Process (LSIP) to conduct a 'Real-Time Strategic Change (RTSC).' It is a powerful process to design and implement change (to align with the overall strategy of the organisation) through the 100% involvement of the employees. The plan was:

- Form a Design Team consisting of staff and workers, who will be briefed by me

- The Design Team will interact with all other employees regarding the RTSC Agenda, the formation of Max Mix Teams and the preparations they needed to make before the event

- Hold a one-day RTSC Workshop to discuss and finalise Action Plans

Vasan spoke to the KMT to decide the date. However, the union leaders (by this time Marico Kanjikode had multiple unions) insisted that any workshops would be held after their COD was discussed and met. Now that would have meant an indefinite delay.

At this time, I told Vasan to tell the Unions that I would be facilitating the RTSC, and I could do it only before the end of June 2002, after which I was not available. I had a feeling that my past equity with them should make them change their stand and it did. I was really very happy when Vasan told me that they had agreed.

After that, we planned and executed the workshop. I must say that it was one of the most useful RTSC workshops I conducted. There was so much cooperation and commitment from the participants. A few weeks later, Raju wrote to me about the effectiveness of the RTSC Workshop. The Unions agreed to shift certain equipment, which they were earlier opposed to. Further, they worked on action plans to improve productivity.

I felt happy that even after many years, the bond was strong. Even today, I keep getting positive messages from those people through social media. However, the presence of Unions made me a bit sad. What must have gone wrong over the years that the workers felt a need to form unions?

I spoke to some employees, and one of the reasons I could identify was a dilution of House activities. Though the House Coordinators are elected and draw plans for the year, what seems to be missing is the rigour.

What Do Some of Them Say?

The culture building at the Kerala factory has touched the lives of many, who found it a career-shaping experience. As I was coming to the end of this book, I talked to some of the people who were associated with the Kanjikode factory. Every one of them had fond memories of those days. Some of them, who are still active in the corporate world, said that they considered the Kanjikode experience great learning. I will mention a few here.

1. **Salil Raghavan,** then Manager HR & TQM, now Head HR at Great Eastern Shipping.

   *"My dissertation while graduating from XL in 1992 was on **Semco,** a Utopian workplace created by the legend Ricardo Semler who wrote **Maverick.** I never thought that three years later I will be a part of a similar journey in a quaint little place in my home State—God's own country. I joined the Kanjikode Plant in rather unfortunate circumstances—my batch mate Suraj died in a tragic accident in March 1995. Marico was the company I wanted to join during Campus placement, so the opportunity came to me three years later."*

   "The guiding light was the Kanjikode Vision modelled around some of the principles from Fifth Discipline of Peter Senge, led from the front by an inspirational Ghanshyam. It was an arduous journey, a road less travelled—but exciting and enjoyable. We created something different and refreshing—there were moments of frustrations, setbacks—but overall it was a wonderful learning experience. We were able to achieve what we set out to do. Some of the unique experiments in HR were

initiated in Kanjikode—the House System, Job Rotations, Jury, Multi-rater appraisal, Kaizen and SGAs. Looking back, it was really the high point of my career."

2. **Nagabhushan Iyer,** then Quality Assurance Manager, now a key Vendor to Marico

Nagabhushan Iyer, fondly called Nagu, was one of the members of the KMT. He was in my team in Marico Jalgaon. He enthusiastically participated in the culture building initiatives in Jalgaon. So, when I moved to Kerala, I wanted him to join my team.

Nagu played a great role in everything that we did at the Kerala factory. Not only was he a go-getter, but he also excelled in dealing with people. He was a fast learner. When we asked him to take up the role of Plant Quality Assurance (PQA), he took the challenge and did a great job of setting up the Quality Systems. Today, he is one of the most preferred business partners of Marico, having established multiple factories for supplying high-quality bottles for the flagship brand, PCNO.

Here is what Nagu has to say about his association with Marico and its Kanjikode Plant:

"When I visited the Kanjikode site along with late Suraj Aravind, I fell in love with it. With the backdrop of mountains, it looked beautiful. Soon, we got completely engrossed in the project work."

"The one thing that touched my heart was Marico's culture. It was very caring and supportive. I experienced it in the way the Top Management interacted with me. I can still remember those moments when Mr. Shreekant Gupte, Vice President Operations, had a long chat with me on acquisition and application of knowledge. Then there were priceless moments with Mr. Harsh Mariwala, Managing Director, when I experienced care and concern for my family and me.

These experiences helped me strengthen my own belief in creating a great work culture."

"My own career took shape as I got the opportunity to head the PQA. It was a great learning experience for me. One of my roles was to facilitate the daily meeting of KMT, which not only resolved operations related issues but also discussed various issues related to the work culture."

"As time passed, there came a time when further promotions seemed unlikely. My work and my ethos were highly regarded by the company, but I felt I did not have the glamour of an MBA. At that time, Mr. Ghanshyam Pant, our General Manager (Works), after discussions with the Top Management, offered me the opportunity to become a Vendor to supply empty bottles. After various discussions, I made up my mind but I did not have any funds. At this point, Mr. Raj Aggarwal, who had just taken charge as Vice President Operations from Mr. Gupte, offered me a company loan to start the business. The support from my family, Mr. Pant and my colleagues finally tilted the scale in favour of taking up the offer."

"I resigned from Marico in January 1996 and started a blow moulding and printing unit with two machines at Coimbatore with a capacity of eight lakh bottles per month. Soon, I had established my unit with maximum productivity and zero wastage of HDPE resulting in huge savings for Marico. My Unit received Best Quality & Productivity Award. Based on my performance I was given opportunities for expanding my operations in Dharwad. In due course of time, I consolidated my operations in Pondicherry and Avinashi. I am proud to say that today I am one of the major Vendors of Marico."

"All these years I have tried to apply the learnings from Marico and tried to inculcate a culture of integrity, honesty, care, indiscrimination, learning, continuous improvement, innovation, and cost-effectiveness."

3. **Srinath Rao,** then Production Manager, now an SAP professional at Accenture, USA

   "I began my Kanjikode stint with trepidations. An apprehension about the Kerala labour force, naiveté about Coconut oil processing and non-familiarity with the language, being the key factors that contributed to this state of mind. Apart from a unique manufacturing setup, Marico had introduced other interesting initiatives at Kanjikode. The 'House System' modelled on schools was a fun experience. Implementing TQM at a factory which was grappling with teething problems was a bold move. I must confess that I was overwhelmed in trying to juggle multiple responsibilities. However, this aspect of the job readied me to accept new challenges when I changed my career trajectory. Never had I been accountable for numerous new responsibilities. Here I was not only heading manufacturing but also dealing with local spare part vendors, conceptualising a new computer-based system, spearheading TQM groups and so on!"

   "Despite a very trying year, the sense of achievement was unparalleled. Having ironed out the shop floor kinks, the team tasted success by way of improved oil mill outputs and efficient bottling line operations. Personally, this was very gratifying as we applied first principles to resolve several of the issues. It boosted self-confidence."

   "Looking back at my relatively short stint of 13 months, I am convinced that no other job provided this level of satisfaction. This experience had convinced me that if I returned to India, I would like to rejoin Marico. I would credit the leadership team for providing me an opportunity to put my best foot, rather feet, forward!"

4. **Pankaj Agarwal,** Vice President – Operational Excellence, Lupin Limited. Pankaj was Production Manager after Srinath Rao resigned. He still considers the Kanjikode experience career shaping and unforgettable.

"Two-way communication was the strongest mechanism to communicate change and build consensus. I personally (a non-Malayalee who could not speak Malayalam) used to communicate at the intersection of A and B shifts and for critical communications—come to the factory at 10 p.m. to communicate with C shift. Communication needed to be clear and consistent, and any changes in decisions had to be communicated clearly with rationale."

"We had critical decisions like relocating copra cutter and who mans the cutter located outside the oil mill building, how do we make changes to shifting of oil and 'Bagda' copra particles in oil, how do we semi-automate expeller feeding process and remove two persons per shift. All these decisions were with associate involvement and with no addition of people. In fact, places where work was eliminated, people were removed from day one. There was never a need for prolonged negotiations."

"Kerala was and is known for frequent 'Bandhs' – 12-hour shutdown to protest against issues of public interest. On those days we used to come into the factory before 6 a.m. and stayed for 12 hours. Workers cooperated and let the oil mill run by working on 12-hour shift. I recall an interesting incident when after the Goa factory had come up and we did not need production from the Plant. On one of the Bandh days, it was decided that we shall shut down the Plant and restart. Workmen associates were of the view that the Bandh will not be enforced as much and the Plant should run. However, the management decision of shutting down the Plant was forced. It was not liked by associates and they did not turn up for starting the Plant in the night. The situation was resolved by me personally going to all shift meetings (two in oil mill, including night and one in packing) and apologised for not taking the right decision. This incident taught me that one should not take people for granted and need for change in organisation requirement should be communicated and given some time to implement, rather than making an overnight affair."

Then there were those who came later and found the experience enriching. Syamaprasad Lakkaraju was one such person. He took charge of the Kanjikode Plant in the year 2001, and then went on to become Executive Vice President of Supply Chain at Marico, before moving on to Britannia and Dr. Reddy's Lab as Director Operations. He still recalls his experience at the Kanjikode Plant.

"The flexibility built in the Kanjikode Plant was unique. While other factories faced a rigid work culture, here was one factory where changes could be introduced quickly. The workforce was always willing to listen and contribute. One could see the family-type bondage and a higher sense of ownership. We could feel everyone as a member of one Marico Kanjikode family."

"When I moved to other companies, I used to cite the example of the work culture at the Kanjikode Plant."

In the end, I would like to quote Shreekant Gupte. Shreekant became the CEO of one of the SBUs of Marico, before moving to Piramal Enterprises as Group President. Since 2007, he has been working independently as a CEO Coach, sharing his rich experience in shaping other companies. About his experience of setting up the Kerala factory, he says:

"The Kanjikode experience helped shape me (as evidently it helped shape almost everyone in our team). Some of my personal learning from Kanjikode go well beyond factory management."

- *Dare to dream big—"set an orbit shifting challenge"—strive to become insanely great.*
- *Avoid the gravitational pull of "current reality."*
- *Don't be "practical." Learn to walk alone.*
- *Have confidence in yourself; you can achieve anything you want—you must want it badly enough.*
- *Challenge the paradigms—industry, company & your paradigms.*

- *Enrol everyone around you. Inspire, excite, cajole, coerce—make it a shared dream.*

- *Never, never, never dilute the dream.*

- *Keep innovating around the obstacles.*

- *The potential to create history is in every one of us.*

- *The problem (& solution) is not "out there", it is "in here" (in your own heart).*

- *You cannot duplicate this by 'cut & paste.' There has to be a strong underlying belief system.*

I say to myself, if these people even after so many years still remember their association with the Kanjikode factory and still find that experience relevant, then it is worthwhile to share the entire story through this book. All the effort that has gone in completing this book is therefore meaningful!

www.ingramcontent.com/pod-product-compliance
Lightning Source LLC
Chambersburg PA
CBHW020922180526
45163CB00007B/2848